The Religions of Mongolia

THE RELIGIONS
OF MONGOLIA

WALTHER HEISSIG

Translated from the German edition by

GEOFFREY SAMUEL

University of California Press
Berkeley and Los Angeles

University of California Press
Berkeley and Los Angeles, California
English translation © *Routledge & Kegan Paul Ltd 1980*
First published as Die Religionen der Mongolei
in Die Religionen Tibets und der Mongolei
by Giuseppe Tucci and Walther Heissig
© *1970 W. Kohlhammer GmbH, Stuttgart Berlin Köln Mainz*

ISBN 0-520-03857-6

Printed in Great Britain

To N. N. Poppe
in respect and gratitude

CONTENTS

PREFACE

In 1846 the young Buryat Mongol scholar Dorji Banzarov undertook, in his book *The Black Faith or Shamanism among the Mongols (Chernaya vyera ili shamanstvo u mongolov)* which appeared in Kazan in the Russian language, to direct attention to the existence in Mongolia of religious forms which had more ancient roots in that country than had Buddhism. The forms of Northern Buddhism in Mongolia correspond in principle to those of Tibet from which they originated, and which Professor Tucci has both described and explained in an exhaustive manner in *The Religions of Tibet* (Routledge & Kegan Paul, 1979). The task which remains, then, apart from a short description of the spread of Buddhism in Mongolia, is only that of describing these beliefs and concepts which belong to the non-Buddhist folk religion of the Mongols. During the more than one hundred and twenty years which have passed since the appearance of Banzarov's book, abundant material has become known in the form of original Mongolian texts and descriptions. Mongolian scholars such as B. Rinchen, B. Sodnam, C. Sodnom, D. Cerensodnom, M. Gaadamba, Manijab and others have in the last ten years made available texts and documents unknown until now; in addition my own researches in European libraries have produced more than seventy-eight manuscripts, containing prayers from the folk religion, invocations and so on, which result from the attentiveness, and enthusiasm for collecting, of Western scholars and travellers. These also in fact supply essential material on the non-Buddhist religious conceptions of the Mongols. I collected these seventy-eight works as preparatory work to the present account, and in 1966, thanks to the interest of Dr Wolfgang Voigt, the editor and initiator of the cataloguing of the Oriental manuscripts of Germany, they were also edited in transcription (Heissig, 1966a). Thus this account is based, in the first place, on philological work on the Mongol texts; work in other languages is given only secondary consideration. My description is therefore only an inventory of the sources today known and accessible, and it is derived from these sources. The wish which Dorǰi Banzarov expressed in 1846 for a 'systematic and *complete* work' on the 'Black' Faith is thus still far from being fully met, but we hope to have taken a step further towards the systematization of the phenomena. What is described here is no longer living in Mongolia; only its last relics can still be observed. This, however, makes understanding it that much more important.

My thanks are due above all to my students, whose lively interest in the ancient religious conceptions of the Mongols has constantly stimulated me to continue working on these materials; they are due to all those who made materials and manuscripts available to me, but especially to the Ethnographic Division of the National Museum in Copenhagen, the Rijksmuseum of Ethnography at Leiden and the Portheim Foundation of Heidelberg; to Prof. Dr Walter Fuchs of Cologne, who kindly placed at my disposal sources for the illustrations, and to Frau Anne Blume of Cologne for her intelligent and careful drawing of these illustrations. That I owe gratitude to the editor and publisher needs no underlining.

If my attempt stimulates further research, then my labour will have been rewarded.

Already in my student days, more than thirty years ago, the works of N. N. Poppe, the old master of Mongolian studies, on the fire-cult and the 'shamanistic' manuscripts of the Mongols awoke in me the desire to understand this matter more clearly. May I be allowed then, in all modesty, to dedicate this work to him.

Bonn, 11 June 1969   W. Heissig

NOTE ON MONGOLIAN
PRONUNCIATION

It is to be noted concerning the pronunciation of words in the
Mongolian literary language that c corresponds to ts, j to dz, γ to
gh and q to kh.

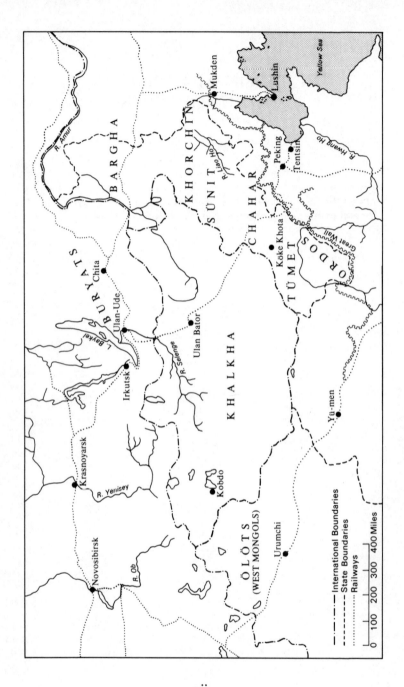

xii

ONE

LAMAISM AND FOLK RELIGION AMONG THE MONGOLS

In the nineteenth century there were about 1,200 Lamaist temples and monasteries in Inner Mongolia, the parts of Mongolia today incorporated into the People's Republic of China, and more than 700 in Outer Mongolia, the territory of the present-day Mongolian People's Republic.[1] A son from practically every family belonged to the clergy; it comprised about one-third of the entire population. Before 1900 there were altogether 243 incarnate lamas living in the territories of the Mongols; of these, 157 resided in Inner Mongolia alone. The politics of the Manchu Empire had drawn the most important of these lamas to the capital, Peking. These figures document sufficiently the fact that in the nineteenth century Buddhism, in its Lamaistic version, was predominant among the Mongols. A description of Lamaism among the Mongols would much resemble one of Lamaism in Tibet, for Lamaism in Mongolia remained spiritually dependent on Tibet, faithful to orthodox Lamaism. It is true that Mongolian lamas wrote significant theological works, but all this happened within the doctrinal structure of the Lamaist church, and in the Tibetan language, and represented no special theological development.

A new development did take place, however, as a consequence of the contact of Lamaism with the old religious concepts of the Mongols. Old forms were taken up, modified and systematized through incorporation into a special literature in the Mongolian language. The development which Giuseppe Tucci has pertinently analysed in the following manner for Tibet repeated itself with regard to the special circumstances of Mongolia:

> When Buddhism became victorious these primitive gods did not vanish; some remained as ancestors of the aristocracy . . . others were transformed into Buddhist deities and received through a nominal conversion the task of guarding the temples or of watching over the sacred character of vows . . . .[2]

On the subject of the enrichment of the Lamaist pantheon by local gods, Tucci remarks:

In practice the circle of the *Sa bdag* (Lords of the Earth) and *Klu* (Dragons) is always open to new recruits. It grew through continual new acquisitions as Lamaism came into contact with new peoples, became conscious of their religious experiences and attempted to adapt these to fit its own premises; in this way pre-Buddhist cults received the mantle of orthodoxy . . . .[3]

In this meeting of Lamaism with the old religious forms of the Mongols, in their influence on Lamaism and their further evolution under the oppression by Lamaism of the Mongolian folk religion, lies what is unique in Mongolian religious history, and what requires description here.

Lamaism had first of all to confront the ecstatic shamanism of the Mongols. The bearers of this tradition were the shamans of both sexes who had the position of priests, called *böge*, 'shaman', and *iduyan*, 'shamaness'. This shamanism was not the personal affair of particular individuals; it was a question of a clearly drawn system of beliefs that was organized in the fashion of a church. It is still recorded for the late sixteenth century that the shamans held council to deliberate on important problems – for example, the news of the approach of a Buddhist missionary.[4] In addition, the similarity of the religious conceptions, and the naming of the same divinities, in the shamanistic prayers coming from Southern Mongolia, from Chahar, Ordos and Buryat Mongolia, as well as in the shamans' songs from Eastern Mongolia, speaks for the existence of a mode of religious thought organized in a definite fashion. The hymns and songs of invocation (*dayudalya*) of this ecstatic shamanism were passed on by word of mouth alone, and that only after they had accepted, under the pressure of Lamaist persecution, Buddhist phrases and figures from the Lamaist pantheon. In the hymns themselves are found allusions to the fact that shamanism is a faith without scripture, a faith without books.

> My Master, you who have given [to me]
> the doctrine without writing!
> My Master, you who have taught [me]
> the doctrine without books,[5]

is from the invocation of the East Mongolian shaman J̌angča Böge, and another East Mongolian shaman, Ügedelegüü Böge, sings likewise:

> . . . You my three Masters, he, hi, hi!
> With my unwritten doctrine, he, hi, hi![6]

2

A Buryat description of the shaman's doctrine, given in a chronicle written in the nineteenth century by Wangdan Yumčung,[7] says:

> People who belong to the religion of the shamans have never had any kind of religious scriptures of their own; all teaching and instruction is given orally and learnt by heart, in the same way that it will be further transmitted by tradition.

Cases of agreement between shaman's hymns that come from the same geographic zone of diffusion indicate the existence of a common school and of transmission from teacher to followers.[8] The involuntary speaking and singing of the shaman, constrained by the 'spirit', which is reported for parts of the classic shamanism of Siberia[9] is not met with here.

In view of the persistent persecution of shamanism by Lamaism in the sixteenth and seventeenth centuries, shamanism found it necessary to camouflage itself by adopting Lamaistic preambles, and also gods from the Lamaist pantheon, and by using the phraseology of Lamaist prayers.[10] In the course of time there developed in this way alongside the pure hymns of ecstatic shamanism those of a 'mixed' type and finally those of a fully 'Lamaized' type.[11]

Alongside these forms of ecstatic shamanism there was, however, a large group of manifestations of religious life which did not involve the shamans as performers, but were the concern of individuals or of the social group involved, the clan or the family. These too (like shamanism itself) reached back into the mists of antiquity; and they too were supposed to summon the protection of the gods. The cult of the eternal blue sky, the veneration of fire, the invocation of Geser Khan and the veneration of the ancestor of the princely family, Činggis Khan, incense offerings in general to the *tngri* (heavenly beings) as well as prayers to hills and mountains and to the powers which dwelt within them, all these belonged in this class of religious activities, as did blessings and curses.[12] By contrast however with the hymns of ecstatic shamanism, the prayers of this 'folk religion' of Mongolia were written down centuries ago. Dorži Banzarov, the Buryat scholar who died at an early age after accomplishing pioneer work in the investigation of Mongolian shamanism, believed that he had discovered the reason for the literary existence of manifestations of Mongolian folk religion in Lamaism's attempt at a syncretistic incorporation of them. He wrote in 1846: 'the lamas have collected the popular prayers and in part added new sections to them in the manner of Buddhism. This however is the reason why we still possess today portions of the old mythology in written form . . .'[13]

Dorži Banzarov's statement is accurate, however, only with

respect to the period of activity of the first *lCang skya* Khutukhtu and, above all, of the Mergen Diyanči-yin Gegen *Blo bzang bstan pa'i rgyal mtshan* and his attempts in the eighteenth century to create a national liturgy in the Mongolian language.[14] A larger number of the folk-religious prayers of this kind are much older than the eighteenth century and show no traces of either Lamaistic reworking or of camouflage necessitated by the Lamaist persecution. In other words, these prayers of an old Mongolian folk religion were fixed in writing before the activity of the lamas, before that is the second period of missionary activity in the seventeenth century. In a description of Mongolian religious forms and beliefs it is absolutely necessary to include these prayers within the material to be investigated, indeed they make up an essential part of the available evidence on the religious life and thought of the Mongols.

As a consequence of the geographical situation of Mongolia as a corridor through which cultures moved, many foreign influences acted upon Mongolian religiosity. Much of a foreign nature was adopted. The Mongols had already come into contact with Buddhism long before the first conversion to Lamaism reported in historical sources. Fo T'u-teng and other Chinese monks had already converted the Chinese-Hunnish border population of North China in the early part of the fourth century AD. The first ideas of Burqan (= Buddha) could date from as early as this period.[15] Buddhist temple-bells with Chinese inscriptions which have been found at sites of the seventh-century Kirghiz kingdom in the region bordering the Yenisei indicate that Buddhist influences in these areas persisted further.[16] In the foundations of the imperial palace built in Karakorum in the thirteenth century remains were found of Buddhist frescoes which came from a Buddhist temple built there previously.[17] The Turkish tribes of the Naiman and of the Kereyid, who participated to a certain degree after their conquest by Činggis Khan in the construction of the Mongolian world empire and in the coming into being of the ethnic group of the Mongols, were followers of Nestorian Christianity. In the thirteenth and fourteenth centuries there were Catholic Christians among the Mongols of central and southern Mongolia. Remains of the Gothic church which the archbishop of Peking, John of Montecorvino, constructed in the thirteenth century for Prince George of the Onggut tribe, a convert from Nestorianism to Catholicism, have been uncovered in southern Mongolia.[18] Besides, remnants of Christian beliefs survived among the Ordos Mongols into the middle of this century.[19] Through close contact with the Turkic Uighurs settled in the cities, who practised Buddhism, Manichaeism and Nestorianism, ideas originating from these religions penetrated among the Mongols, above all Manichaean concepts of light, the figure of Hormusta, the Ahuramazda of the Persians, the thirty-three *tngri* (heavenly beings). The close commercial relations of the Mongols of the thirteenth century with the Near East, the predominant position of men of the Near East in the Mongolian Empire after the military advance of the Mongols to the West brought further influences from Islam, which were then joined by others resulting from the firm implantation of Buddhism in the thirteenth and fourteenth century. All this resulted early on in a predominance of syncretistic thought: analogous traits of different deities, of different religions led to the fusion of the deities. Thus for example, according to a contemporary report, the Mohammedans and Christians of the Mongol period referred to the Buddhist Sakyamuni as Adam.[20]

The indigenous religious conceptions of the Mongols, and the so-called shamanism, was exposed to all these influences from the great religions. One cannot hope to describe this process in its chronological order because of the absence of old sources. A Mongolian account of the origin of shamanism among the Chahar Mongols says, regarding the many forms of Mongolian folk religion besides ecstatic shamanism:

> Apart from these some worship the wind. Others, again, join together tamarisks in the form of a cross and make sacrifices [to this]. Another group put food and drink in a felt bag and worship [this], while others [yet again] make a figure, in which they make a horse and a man out of wood, place the man on the horse and put a sword in the hand of the carved wooden man and worship this [figure]. Some make a horse out of copper and brass and sacrifice.[21]

The prayers belonging to these forms of offering are still unknown, although the reference to a worship of the figure of a rider suggests a connection with the cult of Geser Khan and the worship of equestrian deities.[22] Thus we cannot draw a picture of Mongolian religion of a phenomenological kind which will encompass everything and be fully valid. We can however describe, on the basis of the source material accessible at present, the ecstatic shamanism of the Mongols and the development of the most important folk-religious forms as they came to terms with Buddhism from the sixteenth century onwards. Here too, however, description must necessarily predominate over the tracing of the development in detail.

TWO

THE SHAMANISM OF THE MONGOLS

From the very earliest historical reports concerning the Mongols, from the time of their confederation into a state, right through to the reports of present-day travellers, we meet with accounts indicating the presence of a religion whose essential traits are ecstasy and the ability to combat harmful powers and forces and to look into the future in order to interpret and prophesy, through the help of spirits which have been made subservient.

The records of the twelfth and thirteenth centuries, from the time of the political consolidation of the Mongols and the beginnings of the Mongol Empire, give an account of a religious system at the summit of which was the blue or eternal heaven (*köke tngri, möngke tngri*). Similar conceptions of the divine can already be demonstrated for the Huns of the first centuries AD. The mediator with the world of spirits, of the personifications and hypostatizations of natural forces, was the shaman. At first the shaman and the chieftain of the clan or tribe were often identical, in other words the leader of the tribe or lineage also had the quality of a seer and could visit the spirits of the ancestors and the powers of the underground and of this world. The shaman wore a white dress and rode a white horse.[1] The shamans were members, indeed in part leaders, of the aristocracy of the steppes.[2] In spring the offerings to the ancestors were performed by women, or in the presence of women. This function of woman reminds one of traits of Siberian shamanism, where the shaman often presents heterosexual characteristics.

Pole-offerings were made in a special offering-place by members of the lineage only, by suspending meat or horses from poles. This kind of flesh offering is still reported today from the Tungusic populations of North Manchuria and the Amur bend. The cult of high places also reported from other Altaic peoples was already practised by the Mongols of the twelfth century. Mountains and other prominent landmarks were worshipped through offerings out of thanks and also for the prevention of misfortune. The ritual consisted of kneeling nine times with heads uncovered and with

6

one's belt hanging about one's neck.[3] The tradition regarding this, which has been preserved in various forms, recounts that already at that time fixed alliterative invocations of Tngri Ečige, the 'Heavenly Father', were in use. A great festival of religious character was the 'Day of the Red Disc', the summer solstice on the sixteenth day of the first month of summer.[4] There were holy numbers: three, six and nine. The war drums had drum skins made from the hide of a black bull. The same magical concept of the action of the hide of a black bull on one's enemy, whether he be of this-worldly or other-worldly origin, can still be found among the Mongol shamans of today with respect to the exorcistic action of their drums.[5] Fire was holy and was not to be made impure. It possessed a purificatory property. There was a belief in an afterlife in a realm of the dead: companions, servants and animals were killed to go with dead chiefs and nobles into the other life, to accompany and serve them.

The earliest reports on the popular religion of the Mongols of the twelfth and thirteenth centuries all speak of statues of their domestic gods. These were made of felt in human shape and placed on both sides of the entrance to the tent. It was believed that these gods, personified through the felt figures, concerned themselves about the flocks and protected them. 'They make other gods out of little silk rags . . . when such idols are made, the older women are gathered from the neighbouring tents and they make them with great reverence . . .', Plano Carpini reported.[6] The Mongols offered to these idols libations of the first milk of their sheep, goats, cattle and horses. Libations were also made to them before each meal. We are concerned here with the Ongghot figures of shamanism, which Lamaism began to replace with the images of Buddhist deities only in the seventeenth century.

Although the Mongolian emperor and the upper classes had come into contact with Nestorianism, Roman Christianity, Taoism, Confucianism, Chinese Buddhism and Tibetan Lamaism, shamanism was not driven from its dominating position. There are reports right through to the fourteenth century of the activities of court shamans at the court of the Mongolian ruler of China.[7] Shamanism was the predominant form of religion for the broad masses of the Mongolian people until the collapse of Mongolian rule over China and its border regions in 1368, and it remained so afterwards. The Mongolian people as a whole had not been penetrated by any of the high religions, not even by Lamaism in the thirteenth and fourteenth centuries.

There are only scarce indications of the concepts and forms of Mongolian religious life in the fifteenth century. For the sixteenth century, however, the pre-eminence of shamanism is again attested through numerous sources. These include both Chinese reports (such as, for example, the treatise of Hsiao Ta-heng, a high official of the Ming dynasty, who reports for the second half of the sixteenth century in his notes on the northern barbarians that the religion of the idols had spread from the west towards the north of Mongolia[8]) and original Mongolian sources. From these latter sources it can be concluded that, apart from scanty remains and monastic settlements of the unreformed *rNying ma pa*, the so-called 'Red Hat' sect, in northern Mongolia, which went back to the first contact of the Mongols with Lamaism, most of the rest of Mongolia still adhered to shamanism. This is certain for the first half of the sixteenth century for the Ordos region, the adjoining region of the Tümet to the north-east and the entire eastern part of Mongolia. Especially precise information exists for the second half of the sixteenth century from the realm of the Uriangkhai Mongols, as the Mongols of the Liao-tung region and the regions lying further east from it were called during the Ming dynasty. A Mongolian source reports of them that 'in the territory of the Mongolian people in the east those who are dominated by the forces and ideas of this world worship *exclusively* the *tngri*, the Ongghot images, house-gods, and the shamans and shamanesses . . . .'[9]

Identical reports exist for the same period relating to Ongnighut, the ten Khorchin banners,[10] the Dörbet, Jalait and Ghorlos. Bound up with the manifestations of shamanist belief were bloody sacrifices and animals as funerary offerings in the case of the death of a nobleman, and also bloody offerings in honour of the Ongghot, the statues embodying the ancestral spirits, and in honour of the *sülde*, the spirits animating the standards and military insignia; Mongolian and Chinese sources both report these practices. Some sources also speak of bloody sacrifices on the occasion of the ceremonies at the beginning of the new year and of each new month.[11]

Alongside shamanism there still existed at this time unimportant influences from mystical Chinese Taoism in its simple, popular form of magical Taoism.

The actual nature of Mongolian shamanism can be reconstructed from the shamanist hymns and prayers, transmitted orally through the centuries, which have been noted down during the last few decades by field research, if one separates out all that part of the names and conceptions of the gods which derives from the realm of Lamaism. What then remains of the ceremonial songs contains the original religious concepts of the Mongols before their conversion to Lamaism. True shamanism, as one may call these older religious beliefs in contrast to the more recent types of 'mixed' and finally 'Lamaized' shamanism, is shown in this way to have derived from ancestor-worship.

The spirits of the ancestors are worshipped because they promise help against the constant dangers threatened by the powers of nature.

The protection of man and of his property against all dangers and afflictions from illness or other catastrophe brought about by the powers of evil appears to be the primary function of shamanism. To whom, after all, should man address himself, if not to the spirits of his departed forefathers who had obtained mastery over life? Once belief in the ancestral spirits was present, they would again and again be called upon because of the ability they had once demonstrated to defeat the powers of evil. The person invoking them, often the chieftain of the clan himself, takes on a special position, becomes a mediator, for the small individual living community of the pastoral economy, with the forces to which all life is exposed. He offers the only assistance against illnesses and epidemics, for these too are let loose by powers malevolent to man. Thus the position and function of the shaman is explained out of the need of a society at a primitive economic level to guarantee the stability and protection of the elements constituting it and maintaining it, among which are health, life, fire, food, wild animals for hunting, flocks of domestic animals and an abundance of children, the last of which guarantees both the continuity of the family and, especially, the existence of an adequate human labour force. A legend from the Chahar region about the origin of shamanism,[12] which displays no traces of later Lamaist influence, illustrates the concepts originally predominating among the Mongols concerning the ancestor-cult and the necessity of the shaman as mediator. At a time when the Mongols still lived in their ancestral home in northern Khangai there was an old man who already had access to certain magical practices. When he felt his death approaching, he told his son that he would continue to protect him after his death into his later life, if he would bury him with all honour, and make offerings to him at later times as well. The son did this after his father's death and buried him on a high place, the Red Rock. Burial on a high place is a trait which can be followed through the entire history of the Mongols. The example of Ulanhad or Hung-shan, a hill near to the town of Lin-hsi in south-western Manchuria, shows that high-lying places were especially sought after as burial sites. Here various Stone-Age burial sites were found of a mixed population of Tungus and Mongols,[13] which shows into what distant times the memory of Mongolian tradition reaches back. The legend reports further that the son made regular offerings to the dead man of tea, water and milk and spirits at his father's grave on the first, seventh and ninth day of each new moon. At this time the father's spirit became friendly with the Lords of the Earth, the local spirits, and became ever more powerful. Thus he became able to make lightning and hail fall and to cause misfortune. In this manner he placed himself under Ataγa Tngri, one of the oldest and most widely known shamanist deities, who is often thought of as being personally identical with the all-ruling Eternal Sky.[14] When his mother died, the son buried her too in a similar manner in a high place and sacrificed to her too. She also associated as a spirit with the other ancestral spirits and so acquired the power of flying, of controlling clouds, thunder and lightning and also commanding rain and hail. Besides this she could cause misfortune to men and cattle and poison their health and blood. She began to be worshipped as Emegelji Eji, 'the very old grandmother'. The population, which in this way began to feel the might of these two powerful spirits, discussed what they could do to propitiate and pacify them. The spirits were requested through offerings to be merciful. Thereupon the spirit of the dead father entered a man, who began to tremble. From then on he was worshipped as the black protective spirit (Qara Sakiγulsun). The spirit of the dead mother did the same, entering a girl who also began to tremble convulsively. This spirit was from then on worshipped as Emegelji Eji. These two were now able to fly while they were possessed by their protective spirits. Once, when they were in ecstasy and possessed by the spirits, they flew to the burial place of the two ancestors. There they found drums with wooden supports and also head-ornaments made of the feathers of a yellow bird. Both were handed on to them by the protective spirits. When they struck their drums, they flew back and stepped on one tent after another. Striking their drums they sang as they went, 'To help all living beings we bear the golden drums. We have descended from Ataγa Tngri to protect all living beings on this earth.' The people that heard them said that they must indeed be very mighty protective gods. Thereupon the two requested them to be pious and to offer the libations of tea, milk, spirits and water, so that they could protect them from all evil. Thereupon the people called them shaman (*böge*) and shamaness (*niduγan*) and made offerings to them as they requested. Later they made images of them, making the body from the skin of a year-old lamb and its eyes from black berries. They called these images by their names and referred to them as Ongghon.

Thus it emerges from this legend that Mongolian shamanism arose from ancestor-worship. The living were convinced of the need for the powerful protection of the ancestors. Ecstasy and convulsive trembling were the external signs of the shaman. We find similar features in the shamanistic legends from Buryat Mongolia, where

Lamaism began its struggle against shamanism at the latest period, in other words only seriously from the middle of last century. Since, in addition, many South Mongolian and North Mongolian families fled to Buryat Mongolia in the various fratricidal wars in the sixteenth, seventeenth and eighteenth centuries, especially at the time of Ligdan Khan (1604–34) and of Galdan (1645–97), many religious concepts of the North and South Mongols from the sixteenth and seventeenth century have been preserved in the shamanism of the Buryat Mongols.

From the eighteenth century on Buryats have also lived in the Bargha region. Now the Buryat Mongols' legends of the origins of shamanism allow us to recognize a similar protective function as the origin of shamanism. Thus we hear in a legend which is connected with an Ongghon (a protective deity) of the Khori Buryats how two sisters whose uncle has been attacked by magical sickness cured him with the aid of an ox, in other words through the sacrifice of an ox.[15] Similarly we hear in the oath of a newly initiated Buryat Mongol shaman, which was still in use in 1836: 'I go to this and to that people and help against human illness and sorrow, which I exorcise in various ways.'[16] A Buryat Mongol chronicle explains shamanism as an art or method through which one helps living beings. It should be emphasized here, however, that the shaman does not offer this help in order that it will be accounted to him as a merit in a later life, in another world or in a future rebirth, but only in order to bring to another person help in this life. Shamanism thus is a religion bound to specific goals, directed only to the past and the present. Ideas concerning the future are foreign to it. An analysis of those things on account of which the shamanistic gods, the protective spirits, are invoked, will make this even clearer. In shamanistic prayers from Buryat Mongolia and from North and South Mongolia from the last two centuries, one turns to the shamanistic protective spirits and deities exclusively for the safeguarding of material, worldly objects. They are requested to provide food, property, game, livestock, long life, happiness, children, peace and friendship and domestic happiness; their protection is desired against grief, illness, wounds, epidemics, scabs and serpents, against death and the devil, evil spirits, demons, enemies, passions and misfortunes. Often one god is thought of as the lord over a particular illness, he helps against poisoned foods, against illnesses of horses and cattle-plague. This varies from place to place, which can easily be explained in terms of origin from different groups worshipping different ancestors. One can find a decisive proof in the fact that today, that is in the last two hundred years, after shamanism has adopted Lamaistic traits and Lamaism has incorporated shamanistic customs into present-day Lamaist

11

prayers, alongside the scanty remains of the old pantheon of the folk religion there is now a pantheon of Lamaist deities who are again called on for the protection and provision of the same things. The gods have changed, but not the reasons for which one turns to them.

In what now however consist the practices through which the shaman seeks to achieve his saving and protecting activity? The Mongols call them *bögelekü* and *üjmerlekü*. The former is defined in the following way in a Mongolian text: 'to invite the Ongghot [protective spirits], to let them take possession and then to shamanize in their name and to say that [the force of the protective spirit] has taken possession'.[17] The word *üjemerlekü* comes from the Mongolian *üje*, 'to see something'. But in this case it connotes rather divination, prophecy. Behind the word *bögele* (literally translated as 'to shamanize') stands the word *böge*, 'shaman', which we meet again in the old Mongolian title *bägi*. Shamanizing includes the following magical practices: (a) influence in favour of a sick or aged person through worship, sacrifice or invocation in relation to a particular Ongghot, in order to relieve illness or the danger of death; (b) 'exorcism' of a demon who is arousing evil or illness. This exorcism is based on the idea that the shaman can set his protective spirit to fight against the demon. The exorcism takes place through banishing the demon into either a substitute image (*joliγ*), which is then burned, or into a living animal, which is then slaughtered; (c) 'expulsion' (*γarγayal*), which is performed when misfortune strikes property, living or dead. It should be emphasized that the Mongols distinguish here between 'exorcism' in the case of people and 'expulsion' in the case of animals and objects; (d) the recitation of blessings and magical formulae over herds, children, hunters and so on, in order to protect them from illness, misfortune and such, and to bring them good fortune, blessing and so forth; (e) prophecy using the shoulder-blade of a sheep.

These combinations of this-worldly techniques were used as religious methods by Mongolian shamanism, which thus appears primarily, as has already been remarked several times, as preventative and healing magic.

The demonic powers which were combated were invisible. The positive and protective forces used by the shaman, on the other hand, were represented in the form of figures, which could be given life through the assistance of the shaman as medium. These figures are the Ongghot idols, already mentioned for the Mongols of the time of Činggis Khan. The Emegelji Eji, the figures of the household protective spirit made of felt and silk, which Plano Carpini and Marco Polo already knew, occur in the Chahar shaman legends and are attested as 'Immegildschin' in the eighteenth century by P. S.

Pallas among the Volga Kalmuks.[18] Alongside these figures of household gods which protected the family, there were many others, who were conceived of as the particular protective spirits of cattle, of horses, of the landscape. There are many different accounts of their appearance, but they agree on the main features. In this connection we have, first of all, the descriptions by European travellers which have already been cited. These portray the figures as made from skin and leather, and also partly from strips of silk and cloth. Thus a water-colour of a Buryat yurt made in 1805 by a Dr J. Rehmann, a medical man born in 1753 in Freiburg/Breisgau who travelled into Mongolia in the suite of the Russian prince Golovkin, shows such a domestic god hanging from the supports of the yurt.[19] This agrees in essentials with the description in the shamans' legends. In the National Museum in Copenhagen one can find figures of this kind made out of black skin, which the shaman carried about with him in a leather pouch. These figures are mostly carved figurines of wood or felt which only roughly resemble a human shape. They are mostly kept in little wooden boxes which are attached to a pole of the yurt, or else they are kept in a bag which is hung in the yurt like a cradle. Their size varies, but in general three or so will fit into a wooden box

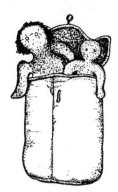

1   Ongghot dolls of felt (Chahar: National Museum, Copenhagen)

20 cm. by 30 cm. (8 by 12 inches) in size; this is confirmed by the oldest of these images, brought by a European traveller in the eighteenth century. Often, however, especially among the Buryats, they are painted on multicoloured silk cloths. Whether one is already dealing here with a consequence of the Lamaist persecution of shamanism (a painted image of this kind could be more easily hidden than the Ongghot figurines) is not entirely clear. This interpretation is contradicted by the fact that European travellers of the thirteenth century already report such idols made out of scraps

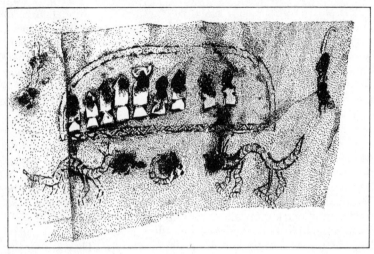

2 Buryat Ongghot painting with metal figures

of silk. Often, however, figurines carved from wood are attached to leather or silk. Among the Buryats the Ongghot paintings are always executed in red. Whether they are on wood, cloth or leather, a thin metal figurine is then attached which represents the soul of the Ongghot. The Ongghot are a figurative representation of the protective spirits.

One can also find, mostly among East Mongolian shamans, bronze figurines from the period of the Animal Style used as Ongghot figures.[20]

A Mongolian tradition has this to say about these protective spirits: 'The souls of shamans and shamanesses who died long ago became the Lords, Ongghot, that is protective spirits and demons, of these mountains, streams, lakes and brooks and forests, and they are both helpful and harmful to living beings.'[21]

A similar, but in part even more precise, definition of these Ongghot protective spirits is found in another Buryat chronicle, in which is said: 'The souls of shamans and shamanesses who have died before and also the souls of other dead people become Ongghot. They call forth illness and death on the living. The souls of other dead people however become demons (*čidkür*) which bring evil to the living.'[22] In connection with many of the Ongghot, Mongol tradition hands down origin-stories in which particular animals often play a role. Here we apparently have something similar to a totemic animal of a clan.

3   Bronze Ongghot

Alongside the Ongghot and the *tngri* (heavenly powers), the shamans also worship a middle level of spirits which are called Buumal (*baγumal*), 'those who have descended'. The origin of this kind of spirit cannot be seen very clearly, but they too doubtless represent a particular category of spirits of kinsfolk. In relation to these spirits also detailed origin-stories are told and transmitted from generation to generation.

The shamans, then, fought, with the help of the Ongghot, which they considered to be favourable to them, against those other powers which had caused suffering or damage to some third person. These destructive powers are either Ongghot, especially evil men (that is the souls of evil men) who cause evil or bring illness and which the shaman must now fight with the aid of his own protective spirits, or else a further, clearly distinct group of evil forces. These evil forces, which the shamanists fear, and which the shamans combat with the aid of the Ongghot they command, are the following: demons, devils or demonic possession (*čidkün*), possession or misfortune (*tüidker*), and also the *ada*, demons which are thought of as soaring in the sky and which surprise men, spread illnesses and awaken desires, the *eliye*, bird-like devils who announce and also bring misfortune; *albin*, wandering lights; *kölčin*, who appear as ghosts of repellent, terrifying appearance; and the *teyirang*-demons. The many kinds of misfortunes and illnesses are individually assigned to these various evil powers. The shamans and their adherents recognize a shamanistic pantheon which extends from the *tngri*, the heavenly beings, through the Ongghot, ancestral protective spirits, Buumal, spirits of other dead relatives, to the various personifications of evil. These personifications of good and evil forces differ substantially from place to place, for each shaman and each place has his or its own local protective spirits. The shamanistic power was stronger if the shaman could point to many generations of ancestors who had become Ongghot, and whose spirits had acquired power over many other souls and spirits, which thus stood at his disposal. The idea of inheritance of the Ongghot, the protective spirits, is expressed clearly in the Mongolian literary tradition. Among the shamans, however, this often led to a legendary series of ancestral Ongghot alongside the actual genealogical series of ancestors. Exogamy, which was practised between Mongolian clans and family groups until the most recent period, promoted the movement of these Ongghot concepts from one region to another, and also explains to some extent why a series of mythical shaman ancestors was imagined alongside the genuine series of ancestors.

From what has been said so far it clearly appears, however, that pure shamanism, that is shamanism before its contact with and influencing and reconstruction by Lamaism, lacked the concept of a world beyond in our sense, a world beyond with the attributes of a Hades to which the shaman might have access. The spirits of dead ancestors were thought of, rather, as remaining in this world in their burial places, where they attained power over other similar spirits. These spirits animated all visible objects; the burial places, as the places where the ancestral spirits resided, developed however into cursed places feared by everyone, and only the shaman had access to the souls of the departed. All later ideas of a Hades and such appear to be secondary and to have been taken over from Buddhism.

In what way did the shaman's intercourse with these protective spirits take place? Here one must first of all outline the leading traits of the nature of the Mongolian shaman in general. The wearing of a ceremonial dress, covered with a number of metal plates, was and is common to all shamans. Long strips and mirror-like objects hang from the clothing. The head is covered either with an ornament of feathers, with iron representations of horns or with silk cloths. The most essential emblems of the shaman are a drum and a staff, but these take various forms depending on the region. Ecstasy is common to all the Mongol shamans, and is in most cases artificially induced through spinning, drumming and the use of means of intoxication.

The costume of the shaman, that is the ritual clothing worn by the shaman, in general differs in cut and appearance from the normal clothing of the Mongols. The function of this ritual clothing must therefore have been to distinguish its bearer from his ordinary fellow-men, to make him stand out. It is decorated with various ornaments, and as with all ritual clothing each of these ornaments has a particular symbolic significance.

The shamanic clothing is inherited from one shaman to the next, exactly as with the Ongghot statuettes, the idols. One can therefore conclude with certainty that the shamanic costumes that we know are not merely creations from last century but represent the ritual clothing of the shamans as it already was before the penetration of Lamaist ideas through the Lamaist missionary activity. Perhaps the best evidence for this lies in the fact that the shaman's costumes of the Tungusic and Siberian tribes, which for the most part have had no contact with Lamaism, show exactly the same essential character-istics as the Mongolian shaman's costumes known to us. Almost all Mongolian shamanic costumes consist of a kaftan, which unlike the normal Mongolian dress is for the most part not closed at the side, but can be closed up on the backside. This kaftan is ornamented with metallic objects of the most varied kinds. Small pieces of metal and bells are attached to it. Ysbrant-Ides already described a shaman's dress of this kind in the year 1704.[23] The most striking, however, of the shamanistic ornaments are perhaps the little strips in snake form which are fastened on to all the corners and ends of the ornaments. The presence of these strips often indicates that the shaman in his clothing seeks to imitate a bird, so that the long strips of leather or cloth on the sleeves and on the front of the dress would symbolize the feathers, and the strips on the backside would be the bird's tail. Evidently this symbolic bird's dress can be explained through the idea of the shaman's flight. This is only one of the meanings advanced; another, occurring especially among the Buryats, sees in these strips the imitation of serpents. Often there is worn over the shaman's dress proper,|which is in general called *quγaγ*,| in other words 'armour', or *eriyen debel*, 'spotted dress', an apron which consists of tapering strips about 80 cm. (32 inches) long hanging down from a band about 20 cm. (8 inches) wide. The colour of the bands is not uniform, and their number also varies. In one case there are nine black cotton strips, in another there are twenty-one strips which are subdivided in the colours of the rainbow. The name of this apron varies, but it is generally connected with one or another protective animal; in one case the apron was called *kürün eryen bars*, 'brown-spotted tiger', and was meant to imitate a tiger's skin through the brightly coloured arrangement of the strips. There is a close formal connection between this apron, or rather ceremonial apron, and the items of clothing usual in Solon, Manchu and Chinese shamanism. The shamanic ritual of the imperial house of

Manchuria knew a similar pleated, and mostly dark-coloured, apron.[24] Analogous items of clothing are reported by the explorers of Tungusic and Manchu shamanism (Shirokogorov, Rudnev and Stötzner). A picture of a contemporary Manchu shaman, taken around 1930 in Mukden, shows us a corresponding ceremonial apron in use. Here we have to do then with influences on Mongolian

4   Manchu shaman, about 1930 (after a photograph by W. Fuchs, Cologne)

shamanism from the Tungusic–Manchu groups of peoples. However, when investigating such phenomena in the history of religions it is in general never possible to delimit precisely what represents a local development or belongs to a particular period. The influences here interpenetrate too far, the cultural characteristics have become too intermingled. Ethnic groups have transferred and changed their names too much and adopted names of famous earlier groups; individual peoples have changed the regions where they lived too much and taken over traits from their neighbours, too often the defeated have given their religious ideas and cultural characteristics to the victors. It is the same here with shamanism. Much of what appears in Mongolian shamanism has already been mentioned in the reports of the Liao and Kitan shamans, and much which was familiar to the Manchu and Solon peoples has been taken over by the Mongols. When one recalls in this connection that the Kitan in the ninth to eleventh centuries were ethnically the same as the later Manchu, and that on the other hand the Mongols under Činggis Khan were heavily influenced by the Liao and their culture, the circle is closed, and it is clear to anyone who approaches the matter more closely that one can no longer discover here to which ethnic group one should assign one or another religious characteristic, or where it ultimately originated. All that one can do in a scientifically respectable manner is simply to carry out a systematic account of the characteristics which are present.

A feature of all shamanic costumes is a further apron or hanging which consists of a belt-shaped protective piece of leather to which is fastened a certain number of mirrors. Sometimes there are nine of these – the Altaic peoples' sacred number of nine. Even in cases where the rest of the ceremonial dress has already been forgotten, the ceremonial apron and mirror-hanging still play a prominent role. The name of this hanging with the *toli*, the mirrors, is various. It can be called the 'blue cloud-bee' and also the 'mount of the shaman' (*böge-yin külüg*). A shaman once explained to me personally that the white horse of the shamans lived in the mirrors. Often, however, mirrors are also worn on the breast and on the back.

These mirrors have a multiple function. In the first place, the mirrors are meant to frighten evil powers and spirits. Phrases in the shamanistic prayers and invocations refer to this task, as for example 'O my mirror, offered by my mother-sister, red and decorated with dragons, O oppressor of infant demons'.[25] We find early equivalents to this function of the shaman's mirror in the same cultural terrain already on a stone coffin from the Liao period in Luan-feng. There a human figure in relief holds a mirror outwards, from all appearances to frighten away any spirits that might disturb the rest of the dead person. We meet a similar portrayal on a wall-painting in another Liao tomb at Liao-yang.[26] This shamanic custom already existed among the Kitan. A further symbolic function of the shamanistic mirror is that it reflects everything, inside and outside, including the most secret thoughts. Through the power of this mirror the shaman acquires the status of an omniscient being. Finally, the third task of the mirror is to turn away the hostile invisible missiles of the evil powers and thus to protect the shaman from the injuries they cause. These mirror concepts are extremely old and apparently do not belong only to the cultural inheritance of the Mongols. This is already suggested by the visual appearance of the mirror, which generally has the form of the old Han-dynasty Chinese bronze mirror, which was distributed in the last centuries BC and the first centuries AD along the trade-routes to all Central Asian cultures. They are generally smooth on one side, even polished to brilliance, while the reverse side is provided with flower-tendrils, birds and figured ornaments.

Mongolian shamans and shamanesses wear the same dress. In this connection it should be pointed out that the presence of female shamans among the Mongols is documented for the pre-Lamaist period exactly as for male shamans. Among the Mongols, however, the shamans lack the heterosexual traits and emblems which one meets with among the North Asian tribes.

The head-ornament can have the most varied appearance among the Mongolian shamans. There are kinds of helmets with iron horns, as have been reported with reference to various North Asiatic tribes, along with coronets of leather and coloured cloths, which are wrapped about the head. If the horn-like iron coronets on the head-ornaments are meant to indicate a protective animal, a totemic animal, then this concept has been lost among most East Mongolian shamans, among whom the silk cloths predominate. Often these are red in colour. The use of such red ritual headcloths is attested for the Buryats, and also for the Mongols of the Khingan Crest region and

5   Solon shaman with copper mask (National Museum, Copenhagen)

for the Mongol groups in the Ts'ing-hai and in the Tsaidam region. The opinion is advanced from various directions that the shaman's headdress and its respective appearance depends on the rank and the grade of power of the shaman concerned. It is known concerning the Buryats and the tribes of the Bargha region that masks were also worn, though this is being progressively lost to memory. We are informed about their appearance by the dress of a shaman of the half-Mongolian Solon tribes north-east of the River Nonni (cf. Figure 5).[27]

The most important emblems of the shaman's dignity and importance, however, are without doubt the drum and the drum-stick. A leading form is the round drum with the crossways stick. The round drum is the predominant form among the North Asiatics, above all the Eastern Siberian tribes; we find it in particular among the Ostyaks, Yeniseians, Yukagirans, Tungus, Gold and Amur peoples. If it is found today among the Mongolian shamans, then one must conclude that there are connections with those Altaic tribes among whom this drum-form is widespread.

The second form of drum differs from the shaman's drum of the Siberian–Tungusic peoples through the presence of a handle with rattles. A thin goatskin is stretched when wet on to an approximately circular, but often also roughly oval, iron ring. In the lower part the skin has a half-moon-shaped hole through which a 19 cm. (7½ inches)-long handle, also made from iron, is fitted. This runs in a ring, of 9.8 cm. (3⅞ inches) diameter, of 8 mm. (⅓ inch)-thick twisted bar-iron. The handle is wrapped in leather strips (cf. Figure 6).[28] Nine small iron rings of an average diameter of 3.5 cm. (1¼ inches) slide along the ring of the handle, making a rattling sound. Here too the number nine is of symbolic significance. This form of drum shows a number of common characteristics with the drums of the Hsingan-Tungus and Manchu shamans. These too have the opening in the drum-skin, and the rattling rings, although they lack the use of iron and the handle. The drum used by a Manchurian shaman from the general area of Mukden had the same form. Drums of this form and material construction were formerly used by Peking children as toys, according to a 'Mirror of Annual Customs', *Jen-ching Sui-shih-chi*, written by a Manchu.[29] The name used for these drums, 'peace-drum' or 'drums that welcome the New Year', suggests a ritual origin of these drums, probably from the Manchu shamanist ritual. The drum and its sound are connected with ideas of a stag and its call, and also often with that of a bull. Its sound, according to the Mongolian idea, frightens the evil demons and drives them away.

The second important emblem of the shaman is the beating-stick,

6   Chahar shaman with drum with handle (National Museum, Copenhagen)

or, as it is also often called, the shaman's sceptre. Here we can clearly distinguish two forms. One is made out of a stick, the head of which is ornamented by a horse's head while the other end terminates in a carved hoof (cf. Figure 7). Sometimes the middle part of the stick is slightly curved as if it were indicating a saddle; now and then one even finds among Mongolian shamans tiny imitations of stirrups fastened at this point.[30] The function of this staff is to enable the shaman to journey to the imaginary place where the battle with the demons will occur. This journey, the flying or riding on the magical horse, takes place in a state of ecstasy, and so the analogy with the European idea of the witch's broom lies only too close.

The second form of the drum-stick is in the form of a thin rod covered with a snake's skin, from one end of which coloured pieces of cloth hang which are meant to imitate, while the drum is being beaten, the flickering of the snake's tongue and the movement of its body. This stick is also called among many shamans 'the speckled scaly snake'. This beating-stick is primarily found among Mongolian shamans who have or who could have had connections of some kind with Tungusic–Manchurian ethnic groups. The functions of the individual emblems and parts of the shaman's clothing do not always agree, but in every case there are two functions in common;

22

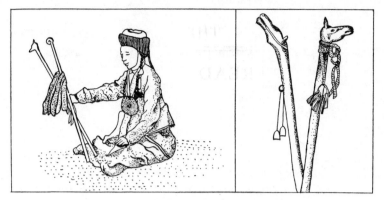

7　Shaman's staffs

first, to make possible the shaman's ride, his release, whether it be through the sceptre or through the mirror-hanging; second, to frighten away evil spirits and demons, whether through the imitation of protective animals, their movements (as with the tongue-movements of the snake), their appearance or their voice. The noise which scares away the demons is always cited as one of the most impressive external aspects of shamanism, and it is already said of the Kitan in Chinese sources that their shamans sought to intimidate the frightened spirits and demons through cries and the sound of bells and also through the noise of sewn-on arrows.

THREE

THE SPREAD OF LAMAISM

The earliest contacts of the Mongols with the Lamaist church in Tibet were primarily political in nature. They came about through the advance of Mongolian military units into the Tibetan border region. In 1247 the Mongolian Prince Godan, returning from a great council of state on the occasion of the coronation of the Emperor Güyüg, met the Tibetan prince of the church *Sa skya Pandita*. On this occasion the lama taught him certain Buddhist doctrines.[1] The first appearance of Lamaist monks from Tibet (members of the *Sa skya pa* sect, close to the *rNying ma pa*, the old, unreformed Tantric sect) at the Mongolian court was caused less by the Mongols' spiritual needs than by the fact that the Mongol emperor of China, Khubilai, wanted to hold a representative of the *Sa skya pa* then ruling Tibet in his vicinity as a pledge for a friendly attitude on Tibet's part. *'Phags pa*, the nephew of *Sa skya Pandita*, thus came to the Mongolian court as a hostage. His adroitness in arousing the interest of the ruling class in his religion led not only to the initiation of Khubilai and of his consort Čamui but to the conversion of at least the court and the ruling class, and to *'Phags pa's* appointment as teacher to the emperor (*Ti-shih*) and teacher to the state (*Kuo-shih*). From the time of *'Phags pa* (1235–80) onwards, *Sa skya* monks were always spiritual advisers of the Mongol emperors in China. The influence of *'Phags pa* particularly affected Emperor Khubilai's ideas of the state, of the connection between church and state, and of the position of the emperor. From an intellectual and religious point of view, the first conversion of the Mongols to Lamaism did not go very deep. It rested, in addition to the necessity for political instruction and advice, on the influence of Tibetan medicine as practised by the Tibetan monks, which proved more convincing to the Mongols than the shamans' prayers for health, and on the greater magical effectiveness of Tantric magic. Marco Polo reported that the monks of the Red sect of Lamaism at the court of Khubilai vied with each other at feats of magic.[2] Until the early fourteenth century they were also competing in this field with the court shamans.[3]

24

During this first Lamaist conversion the cult and worship of the terrifying manifestations of divinity spread among the Mongols. These divine forms included, for example, the wild, flame-surrounded Mahakala (a Lamaist form of Siva) and the guardian deity Hevajra. These Lamaist gods fitted in especially well with the political dynamism of the Mongols and with their militant nature. The demonic character of these gods outstripped that of the local Mongol gods and their ritual contained dreadful sacrificial ceremonies. During the last decades of Yüan rule over China Tantrism in its most secret form of sexual Tantra exercised a great influence on the Mongolian court. The Mongols did not understand the union of the god with his female counterpart (Tib. *yab yum*), which is prescribed in the ritual texts and is to be experienced spiritually by the meditator, in the esoteric manner. Not only Chinese sources but also Mongolian sources describe the orgies celebrated at the Mongol court as the result of the profane misunderstanding of this doctrine, and the degeneration of the Mongolian ruling class which went along with this, as one of the most important causes of the collapse of Mongol rule over China (1368). The broad Mongolian public was not, however, touched by the first Lamaist conversion. Although at the time of the last Mongolian sovereign part of the Lamaist canon was already translated into Mongolian, and foundations of monasteries even took place, while indeed on the other hand a certain proportion of Mongolian families adopted Christianity, shamanism nevertheless remained the characteristic and normal religion of the Mongols even after the collapse of the Mongolian empire in China in 1368. Apart from some misunderstood and degenerated customs, which had developed into mere superstition, and a few forgotten monasteries in the region of North Mongolia, there was until the sixteenth century little, if indeed anything at all, surviving among the Mongols of what had been brought to them by the first contact with Lamaism in the thirteenth century.

The second expansion of Lamaism in the direction of Mongolia did not in its origins rest at all on a firm intention of the Lamaist church in Tibet of extending itself into Mongolia. This time the Lamaist conversion of the Mongols took its origin in a remarkable manner from China, indeed from the China of the Ming dynasty. During the Mongol dynasty the number of Tibetan Lamaist clergy and of their monasteries in China had become very large. They took on a privileged status there. The flight of the Mongols from China in 1368, and the collapse of Mongolian rule, temporarily robbed them of their influence but in no way entirely drove them from China. Thus the remarkable situation came about in the fourteenth century that Lamaism still flourished in China as before, while among the Mongols themselves it had been completely forgotten. Around 1431, four-language collections of *mantras* and *dharanis*, with pictures of the deities, dating from the Yüan dynasty and intended for Mongols also, were still being printed in China. The disappearance of Lamaism in North China was only brought about in the first half of the sixteenth century, by anti-Buddhist and anti-Lamaist movements under the Ming emperors Ying-tsung and Shih-tsung, the latter of whom had a special predilection for Taoism. It appears that in the course of this persecution Tibetan monks sought refuge among the Mongols and established themselves there.[4] The first references to the arrival of Lamaist monks among the Mongols of the Sino-Mongolian border region occur for 1547.[5] The West Mongolian tribes of the Ölöts and the Oirats admittedly must by this time have been already firmly under the spell of Lamaism, for Neyiči Toyin, the apostle of Lamaism among the Eastern Mongols, who was born the son of a west Mongolian prince of the Torghuts, along with many of his contemporaries, saw his highest goal as that of renouncing the world and becoming a Lamaist monk.[6]

Military raids of the Tümet prince Altan Khan in the Kokonor region brought him into closer contact with Tibetan lamas, and from this arose the renewal of missionary activity among the Mongols.

Altan Khan, a descendant of Činggis Khan in the twenty-fifth generation, born in 1506, invited *bSod nams rgya mtsho*, the leader of the Yellow Sect, that is the reformed sect of *Tsong kha pa*, to come to him in Mongolia; he later gave this lama the title of Dalai Lama. At the same time Altan Khan requested the sending of a Tibetan monk from China and the transmission of Buddhist scriptures in the Tibetan language from Peking. The Chinese met his requests, since Wang Ch'ung-ku, a far-seeing governor-general of the frontier region, recognized the possibility of pacifying the Mongols through their conversion to Buddhism. In Tibet they took rather more time, but the Dalai Lama too made the journey to come together with Altan Khan in 1576. His meeting with Altan Khan led to a mass conversion of the Tümet and Ordos Mongols. These tribes adopted at this time a series of new laws which ensured the spread of Lamaism among the Mongols, and simultaneously placed obstacles in the way of the further practice of shamanism. According to the Mongolian chronicles the most important points of the laws adopted at this time were more or less as follows: the killing of women, slaves and animals as funerary offerings, which was practised up to this time, was forbidden. It was further prohibited to slaughter human beings or animals as sacrifices for the yearly, monthly or other regular offerings, and in general all bloody flesh offerings and all blood-offerings were forbidden. The possession of Ongghot was also unlawful, and the order was given for these to be burned. In their place images of the seven-armed Mahakala, the protective lord of Lamaism, were to be worshipped in every yurt. These edicts were proclaimed as binding for the Tümet ruled by Altan Khan from 1577, and for the Ordos Mongols by Dzasakhtu Khan (1558–82). They found rapid acceptance among the South Mongolian tribes, which in the course of a few decades made Lamaism into an essential element of their spiritual life.

Altan Khan, who had originally been just as much given to the dreadful superstitions of his epoch as his contemporaries (it is reported of him that before his conversion to Lamaism he had used for the treatment of his gout the old Mongolian practice[7] of placing his feet in the opened body of a man), brought Lamaism to flower within his domain within a few years. He built the first monasteries in his residence of Köke Khota and its environs. In the course of a few years Köke Khota (Kuei-hua) became a leading centre of Lamaist spirituality and of the Lamaist clergy. In the mountains around the town numerous contemplative ascetics and anchorites gathered with their disciples and servants. Buddhist works were translated from Tibetan into Mongolian. Around 1578 a grandson of Altan Khan had a translation made of the *Suvarnaprabhasa Sutra*, one of the fundamental works of Lamaism. The first translations were written on writing-tablets of polished apple-tree wood following the old practice used in the fourteenth and fifteenth centuries. The wooden tablets were held together by two cords going through them, like the Indian palm-leaf manuscripts.

The new teaching rapidly won over to itself the princes of the Ordos Mongols and soon spread towards the north of Mongolia. Here too the initiative came not from the Lamaist clergy but from Abadai Khan of the Khalkha, who saw in it a boost to his political prestige, and who visited the Dalai Lama during the latter's journey to Mongolia. Concerning this the Mongolian tradition reports: 'In the middle of the mandala of Mahakala the (Dalai) Lama burnt all the idols of the Khan and arranged for the building of temples.'[8]

The meeting of Abadai and the Third Dalai Lama marks the beginning of the spread of reformed Lamaism, that is of Lamaism in the form preached by *Tsong kha pa*, in the territory of the Northern Mongols. In 1586 Abadai built the monastery of Erdeni Juu for the images of gods presented to him by the Dalai Lama. Here too there went hand in hand with this the prohibition of the practice of the old shamanistic forms of religion. For the consecration of the monastery the Dalai Lama sent the *Sa skya* lama *Blo bzang bzang po* as his representative. This lama required from Abadai Khan and the

Khalkha the putting into effect of commandments and prohibitions concerning shamanism similar to those which had been introduced a few years earlier among the Chahar, Tümet and Ordos. In this region, however, monasteries of the unreformed *Sa skya pa*, *Karma pa*, *rNying ma pa* and *Jo nang pa* sects had remained from the time of the Yüan dynasty.[9] In general the conversion of this period, which beginning from Altan Khan encompassed Mongolia to the north and east, was in its first stages not at all the exclusive affair of the 'Yellow', reformed sect. The *Sa skya pa*, whose doctrinal structure stood close to that of the 'Red', unreformed *rNying ma pa*, took a major part in the spiritual and religious life of the Mongols until the decisive advocacy of the Yellow sect by the Khalkha prince Tümengkin[10] and the preference for this sect by the Manchus after 1634. Indeed, in many regions the Yellow, reformed sect prevailed only slowly and with difficulty.

In 1586, the Dalai Lama again visited Mongolia, on the invitation of the Kharchin, who had been reached by the Lamaism radiating from the domain of Altan Khan. On this journey, which resembled a triumphal progress through the regions which had meanwhile been converted, he went into the region of the Kharchin at that period, which extended north-east from Chang-chia-k'ou (Kalgan) in the direction of the old Yüan summer residence of K'ai-p'ing near to the Dolonor and beyond. With him there came a series of Tibetan and Mongolian lama-monks, who now established themselves at the Kharchin court and made this into another important centre of Lamaist development.[11] The Dalai Lama charged these monks not only with translating various works from the Tibetan, but also with preparing the basic *Alikali* textbook on orthography and other grammatical works for the Mongols with regard to further translating work. These tasks were performed at the end of 1587 by a Mongolian translator called Ayusi Guosi. In the process he founded a school of translation which in the course of the following years would be visited by a series of Mongolian monks and also noble laymen. It was these students of Ayusi Guosi who then in the following decades, to the end of the sixteenth century and the beginning of the seventeenth, translated numerous Lamaist works from Tibetan into Mongolian. When the Third Dalai Lama died in 1587 the importance of this conversion of the Mongols had already been recognized in Tibet, the homeland of Lamaism. Thus it came about that a few weeks after the death of the Third Dalai Lama, already in the first month of the year 1588, the Fourth Dalai Lama was reborn in the form of the son of a Khalkha Mongol prince, Sümer Dayičing Qung Tayiji. This newly born head of the entire Lamaist church was immediately taken to Köke Khota, the capital of Altan Khan, for religious training. This is worth noting, and one can conclude from it that this town, which was only founded some years before, had already become a leading centre of the Lamaist religion. Under the protection of the sons and grandsons of Altan Khan, and with the aid of their riches, many monasteries had arisen here. The work of translation flourished. Many monastic teaching centres trained novices for the religious way of life. Among these novices was Neyiči Toyin (1557–1653), a young nobleman from the Torghut tribe, who had renounced his father's house, his lordship and family and gone to Köke Khota to find a theological training there. In the last decades of the sixteenth century there were made here under the leadership of Guosi *chos rje*, one of the most famous translators of the period, translations of the most important works of the Tibetan Lamaist literature into the Mongolian language, including works such as the biography and the *Hundred Thousand Songs* of *Mi la ras pa*, the *mDzang blun*, and the Sanskrit work *Saddharmapundarika*, an essential text of Mahayana Buddhism, and others. This makes plain the significance which Kuei-hua ch'eng (Köke Khota) had as a spiritual centre of the new religious movement which had begun to take hold of Mongolia. The highest of the spiritual leaders there was the *sTong 'khor* Khutukhtu.

The princes won over to Lamaism designated young noblemen in great numbers for the priesthood. Altan Khan had 'a hundred noblemen, princes among them'[12] enter the priestly state in 1578 on the occasion of his first meeting with the Third Dalai Lama. The princes of the four Oirat tribes of West Mongolia promised before 1599 that each prince and nobleman would devote one son to become a clergyman.[13] It is difficult to avoid the impression that part of the conversion consisted in acts of the government. However, it came about in this way that numerous sons of princes and young members of the aristocracy entered the religious way of life. They were educated primarily at *bKra shis lhun po* in Tibet, the seat of the Panchen Lama, who was the second head of the Lamaist church.

At the end of the sixteenth century and the start of the seventeenth the South Mongolian tribes were fully open to Lamaism. Numerous monasteries were built and many pious foundations and commemorative inscriptions erected which mention Altan Khan as a promoter of the Buddhist religion. A find of manuscripts in a ruined stupa in Olon Süme, in the Yüngsiyebü region, which is dated by the stone inscription of 1594 also found there, shows that Lamaist prayers to the Lords of the Earth, for the banishing of demons, were already in use in the Mongolian language, as also were fundamental works such as the *Vajracchedika Sutra*.[14]

At this time Lamaism was carried a little further again towards the east.

The Chahar Mongols, who had already come into contact with Lamaism in the lifetime of Altan Khan, entirely adopted this doctrine. In the second half of the sixteenth century they extended their domain further to the east. Darayisun, a contemporary of Altan Khan, moved from the frontier region of the Ming prefecture of Hsüan-hua, the region around the old Yüan summer residence of K'ai-ping, to the Liao-ho river. The district of Bagha Küriye (in the same area as the present-day Küriye Banner) became his new domain. From this region his successors, up to Ligdan Khan, sought to bring the other Eastern tribes under their domination with the claim that they were the rightful successors to the throne of the Great Khan. In this area, the territory of the present-day Küriye, Khorchin and Kharchin Mongols, Ligdan Khan (1604–34) founded many monasteries. The *Shar ba pandita,* a *Sa skya* monk, was sent to him as a spiritual counsellor, and was with him from 1617 onwards. From 1626 the *Shar ba* Khutukhtu lived in Pai-t'a-tzu in the territory of the present-day Bagharin. There, where the pagoda known as Činčin Čaγan Suburγa stands from the Liao period, Ligdan Khan had further stupas erected in honour of himself and his sister. He renewed the buildings and thus a new monastery arose. The *Shar ba* Khutukhtu, an adherent of an unreformed Lamaist sect, brought about the translation of numerous Lamaist works into Mongolian, and himself wrote a history of the origin of the Mongolian princes. Thus in the years up to 1634 Lamaism flourished in this region too, eastwards from the Hsingan ridge. Between 1628 and 1629, however, one of the greatest spiritual achievements of the Mongols took place in Ligdan Khan's territory. Under the leadership of *Kun dga 'od zer* Mergen Manjusrī Pandita, and a certain Ananda whom we can probably identify on grounds of the similarity of name with the *Shar ba* Pandita, the spiritual counsellor of Ligdan Khan, who was also called Ananda, the Buddhist canon was translated from the Tibetan language into Mongolian by a committee of editors consisting of thirty-five Mongolian and Tibetan scholars. More exactly, all the translations of Lamaist religious texts which had been made since 1580, the beginning of the conversion, as well as translations from the Yüan dynasty, were corrected and revised, those which were missing were translated and the canon brought together in the Mongolian language[15] in 113 volumes. The place where this year-long work of editing was carried out was, according to the knowledge we have so far, probably the temple built by Ligdan Khan in Tsaghan Suburgha. When one considers that in this period of time there were translated, along with the 1,161 works contained in the canon, many others as well, including also those of the Red sect and many Tantric teachings, and when one reflects that for the theological and philosophical literature many new concepts had first to be created in Mongolian, one comes to the conclusion that the Mongols had taken an extraordinary intellectual leap in the fifty years from 1579 to 1629. This leap did not only concern religious literature; it also led to the writing down of a secular history of a different and markedly historical character.

8   The first *rJe btsun dam pa* Khutukhtu (Ondür Gegen, 1635–1723) after a devotional
print from Northern Mongolia (Portheim Foundation, Heidelberg)

In 1635 a son was born to the Khalkha prince Gombudordzi who, as the *rJe btsun dam pa* Khutukhtu, was to become the spiritual prince of the church for Northern Mongolia in Erdeni Juu. After his religious education was completed, he spoke out like his predecessors in the South Mongolian region against the spread of shamanism and the shamanist idols. Under him the Red sect monasteries in the Khalkha region lessened in significance and the Yellow reformed teaching of Lamaism gained ground. Thus at the beginning of the seventeenth century Lamaism was everywhere making progress. Köke Khota, the Kharchin region, the monasteries in the territory of

31

Ligdan Khan, and Yeke Küriye, the seat of the *rJe btsun dam pa* in the Khalkha territory, the present-day Ulanbator of the Mongolian People's Republic, had developed into centres of Lamaist clergy and theology, out of which many lamas wandered throughout Mongolia and missionized its inhabitants. A whole new spiritual epoch had begun for Mongolia. Only in the east of Mongolia, among the tribes in the Liao-tung region and to the east of there did the old religion still hold sway. In the east too there was coming into existence the new power of the Manchu, who would promote the final triumphal march of Lamaism yet further and bring it to its conclusion.

A prince of the Khorchin Mongols at the start of the seventeenth century excused the limited spread of Lamaism among his people, the ten Khorchin tribes, by saying that 'there have been few scholars among us. Nobody is familiar with the holy scriptures, for religion has not yet spread very far.'[16] One of the few early religious visitors was the Third Dalai Lama, who in 1588 had consecrated a temple in the Khorchin territory at the invitation of the Khorchin Khan. Here too, participation in the new religion did not at first go beyond the princely class, and the people preferred 'the shamans and shamanesses, and all worshipped the Ongghot'.[17] Among the neighbouring Dörbet and Jalait too the 'so-called Buddhist faith was completely unknown'.[18] At the beginning of the seventeenth century shamanism held sway in the entire East Mongolian region, from the Ongnighut in the south to the River Nonni in the north. The missionary activity of Neyiči Toyin (1557–1653), a *dGe lugs pa* monk originating from a West Mongolian princely house, and of his disciples, in the years between 1629 and 1653, converted the Mongols living here too to Buddhism, suppressed shamanism for a fairly long time and forced it to hide and to transform itself.[19] An eighteenth-century Mongolian source celebrates this missionary achievement: 'There among the ten banners of the Khorchin his eminence the holy exalted lama first introduced the teaching of *Tsong kha pa*.'[20] The decision by the Manchu dynasty, who came to the Chinese throne in 1644, to secure their domination over China through a pacified frontier region to the north and west brought about the state's support for the Lamaist church. After the defeat and death of the last Mongolian Great Khan, Ligdan Khan (1604–34), the Manchu rulers acquired the succession to him not only with respect to his claim of legal rule over all Mongolia but also his claim to be the 'patron' of Lamaism. This development began with the building of the great Yellow Temple in Mukden (1636–8) for a Mahakala statue, originating from the Yüan dynasty, which had previously belonged to Ligdan Khan.

The Manchu rulers promoted the Lamaist clergy in Mongolia through the building of monasteries and through financial donations.

Emperor K'ang-hsi, brought up in his youth by his grandmother Hsiao-chuang (1613–88), a Khorchin princess, was the first of the Manchu emperors to display a personal religious interest in Lamaism. His son Yung-cheng (1723–35) and his grandson Emperor Ch'ien-lung (1736–95) continued this tradition, in which political good sense went along with genuine religious participation. During this period the Mongolian translating activity flourished. More than 230 translations of Tibetan Buddhist works into Mongolian, and Mongolian theological writings, were promoted between 1650 and 1911 by the Manchu princes, and to a greater extent the Mongolian princes; they were printed in Peking as blockprints and distributed among the Mongols.[21] Between 1718 and 1720 Emperor K'ang-hsi had the Mongolian translation of the Buddhist canon, the Kanjur, printed in 108 volumes in Ligdan Khan's edition and distributed throughout Mongolia. During the regnal period of the Emperor Ch'ien-lung the great collection of commentaries to the Kanjur, the Tenjur, was translated (also with the assistance of older translations, in part from the Yüan period), and it was printed between 1742 and 1749 in 226 volumes.

Numerous Mongolian monasteries were built with Imperial funds, and therefore had a special status. Each separate period of the partly bloody pacification and incorporation into the Manchu empire of the regions of Mongolia, a process which came to a final end with the annihilation of the West Mongolian separatist Amursana in 1756, was marked by Imperial foundations of temples and monasteries. In addition there were the many monasteries founded and endowed by pious noblemen.[22]

From the beginning of their pro-Lamaist policy the Manchu sovereigns sought to administer the Lamaist church in Mongolia from Peking, despite its unequivocal theological connection with Tibet and Lamaism there.[23] For this reason they appointed supreme heads for Inner Mongolia in the person of the *lCang skya* Khutukhtu and for Outer Mongolia in the person of the *rJe btsun dam pa* Khutukhtu. The first *lCang skya* Khutukhtu of Peking, *Ngag dbang blo bzang chos ldan* (1642–1714), was summoned by Emperor K'ang-hsi to Peking for this reason and he was gradually trained for this function.[24] His rebirth *Rol pa'i rdo rje* (1717–86) in particular developed into a key figure in the Manchu religious policy towards the Mongols. In order not to elevate to the rank of prince of the Mongolian church any partisan of the latent aspirations to Mongolian independence, which were always present, the reincarnations of these lamas were most often found in Tibet. In the course of time important reincarnations from Mongolia and from Tibet were called to Peking more and more by the Manchu emperors, and given theological and ecclesiastical administrative offices. In the nineteenth century, alongside the *lCang skya* Khutukhtu, there were the Galdan Siregetü Khutukhtu, who had resided in Peking since 1734, the *A kya* Khutukhtu, the *sTong 'khor*, *rJe drung*, Drimong and *Grags pa* Khutukhtus. Since the presence of a reincarnate lama meant a substantial increase in followers, donations and prestige, the number of reincarnations in Mongolia grew steadily. Before 1900 there were finally 14 reincarnations in Peking, 19 in Northern Mongolia, 157 in Inner Mongolia and 35 in the Kokonor region, making a total of 243.

Despite the administrative and political separation of Mongolian Lamaism from Tibet which was successfully carried out by the Manchu emperors, the spiritual and theological dependence on Tibet remained very close. Although numerous Mongolian lamas made substantial contributions to Lamaist theology, which were significantly all composed not in the Mongolian language but in Tibetan, the church language of Lamaism, the Mongolian theological schools developed no divergent doctrinal interpretations. Only in those cases where, at the instructions of Lhasa and of the Dalai Lama, the Mongolian folk religion was incorporated in a syncretic fashion into the doctrinal edifice of Lamaism, did there take place any truly local development.

For the Mongols, the ever more effective diffusion of Lamaism from the late sixteenth century onwards led to decisive structural changes in society and economy. The creation of the monastic communities, which formed independent economic units, provided the first profound break with the old economic system of the Mongols.[25] The accumulation of property and riches in the monasteries brought them in the course of time into opposition with the nobles, who had previously been the only owners of property, as well as with the propertyless layers of the population. The large number of lamas represented a heavy handicap for the rest of the population. Although the rigid doctrinal structure of Lamaist religion allowed the spiritual development of the Mongols to take place only along the lines laid down by Lamaism, the monasteries with their schools and their training in the various branches of knowledge opened the way notably to a higher level of spirituality for a certain percentage of the Mongols. Education in the monasteries also, however, meant for many other gifted children, not only from the princely class, access to knowledge of the alphabet, to the ability to write and read. The development of the written literature of the Mongols is therefore closely bound up with it. Some of the most important bards and minstrels of the nineteenth century and of the first half of our century were educated in the monasteries and learnt to read there before they entered the lay estate. Without the assistance of learned Lamaist monks the notable Mongolian historiography of the Mongols in the seventeenth to nineteenth centuries would have been inconceivable.[26] Many themes from Tibetan and Indian works reached the Mongols through translations and through the oral teaching of monks, and enriched their treasury of stories.

The building activity and the need to create works of religious art necessitated the development of a class of artisans. The privileged social and economic position of the Lamaist monks, especially of the high clergy, all the same concealed within itself the seeds of the downfall of Lamaism in Mongolia. In the nineteenth century criticism of the misuse of power and of the irreligious behaviour of monks arose from the population and also from among the clergy themselves. The heights of Lamaist philosophy remained the preserve of a few select people; the mass of the monks in the nineteenth century and at the beginning of our century was theologically untrained. The downfall began with the decay of Manchu power. The divergence between preaching and reality was no longer to be bridged. Once political forces took hold of it, this led around the middle of the twentieth century to the end of Lamaism in Mongolia. The Lamaist institutions still present in the Mongolian People's Republic, like those in the Mongolian minority areas of China, are of only symbolic significance.

FOUR

THE LAMAIST SUPPRESSION OF SHAMANISM

Reports of the prohibition of shamanism and of its persecution and suppression by the Lamaist missionaries run like a red thread through the history of the second conversion of the Mongols from the sixteenth century onwards. Anti-shamanist resolutions such as the legislation of Dzasakhtu Khan (1558–82/3) and the edicts of Altan Khan of the Tümet (1557/8), which forbid under threat of punishment the possession of Ongghot figures and their worship through bloody sacrifices, form the prelude. The stimulus for them came from the Third Dalai Lama himself. The shamanist idols were to be replaced by representations of the Buddha and, especially, by such 'terrifying' deities as the six-armed Mahakala. In place of the forbidden shamanist songs and hymns, *dharani* formulae and exorcistic prayers were taught, and spread among the people in numerous copies. Feats of Tantric magic and miraculous healings appealed very much to the princely class; as a result they were able to agree to forbid shamanism.

The biography of Neyiči Toyin (1557–1653), the missionary to the East Mongolian tribes, offers a lively description of this process. When a princess of the Ongnighut was seriously ill around 1629 she was healed by Neyiči Toyin; at the same time he defeated a powerful shaman. The healing of a blinded shaman by Neyiči Toyin is also reported.

The princes of the Khorchin who had been won over to the cause of Neyiči Toyin and to the Lamaist doctrine which he preached made arrangements as a result towards 1636 to promote the spread of the new religion.

All these shamans and shamanesses of the heretical, false religion were caused to renounce the propagation of their Tngri and Ongghot.[1]—In order to begin the spread of the Buddha's doctrine with benevolent intention, the Tüsiyetu Khan of the Khorchin let it be publicly known: 'I will give a horse to whoever learns by heart the summary of the Doctrine, and a cow to whoever can recite the Yamantaka *dharani* by heart!' Thereupon, from the

9   Neyiči toyin after a Peking blockprint of his biography (eighteenth century)

moment that they heard this announcement, all the poor and
have-nots learnt the prayers according to their intellectual capacity.
And since the Khan, as he had announced, gave horses and cows
to those who had already learnt the prayers from other people,
there were many believers . . . .[2]

However Neyiči Toyin acted like his predecessors, above all the
Third Dalai Lama himself, who had always desired the annihilation
of shamanist idols. At around the same time (about 1636) he invited
the Khorchin nobles in an address

> to cease the worship of idols, for this is a great hindrance for your
> eternal salvation . . . . Ruler and nobility became strong believers
> on hearing this address [the biography further reports] and,
> following his words, each sent his own messengers, each accom-
> panied by one of the monks from the lama's following, on post-
> horses in every direction. When these came across the dwellings of
> noblemen, dignitaries and ordinary people, without making any
> distinction, they said 'Give us your idols!', and many gave them to
> them; others, however, too frightened to seize them themselves
> simply said 'There they are'.—Sent out over the whole banner,
> the monks and messengers gathered the idols in and brought them
> together from all sides. What they had gathered together they
> then piled as high as a tent of four folding frames before the
> dwelling of the lama [Neyiči Toyin] and set fire to them.—Thus
> the false religion was brought to its end, and the Buddha's
> doctrine became immaculate.[3]

The comparison of the pyre of assembled Ongghot figures with a Mongolian yurt of four frames enables one to calculate with some accuracy the number of confiscated Ongghot. A normal Mongolian round tent is about 2.40 m. (8 feet) high at its highest point; a *qana*, a folding-frame side-section, is about 2 m. (6 feet 8 inches) long. The pyre accordingly had a circumference of about 8 m. (27 feet) and was up to 2.40 m. (8 feet) high. The size of the confiscated Ongghot figures would scarcely have differed from that of the Ongghot still found today, which are about 25 cm. (10 inches) high.[4] Thus the number of Ongghot collected in the territory of the Khorchin alone must have consisted of several thousand examples.

Around 1650 *Rab 'byams pa* Caya Pandita (1599–1662) took similar measures in the Ili territory, inhabited by West Mongolian tribes, and in North-Western Mongolia. He gave his monks and disciples this instruction: 'Whoever among the people whom you see has worshipped Ongghot, burn their Ongghot and take their horses and sheep. From those who let the shamans and shamanesses perform fumigations, take horses. Fumigate the shamans and shamanesses however with dog dung.'[5]

One can still observe the same kind of Lamaist procedure against shamanism and Ongghot worship in the last decades of the eighteenth century in connection with the spread of Lamaism among the Buryats, the northernmost Mongol group. Although the Buryat tradition reports the presence of Lamaist monks among the Khori Buryats as early as the first third of the seventeenth century,[6] Lamaism did not flourish among the Buryats before 1712. For this year the arrival is reported of the first Lamaist missionaries from Tibet in the Selenga and Khori territory.[7] There the first Lamaist monasteries were founded only in 1730, when more than fifty further Tibetan monks and a hundred Mongolian monks were sent into this region.[8] The Lamaist missionary activity among the Khori Buryats extended from then until 1741.[9] Until 1788 the Agha Buryats were 'complete adherents of the shamanist faith'.[10] Only in 1819 did a monastic assembly of the Conghol monastery decide on the persecution and burning of shamanist idols.[11] From 1820 on 'the Selenga and Khori Buryats, the fifteen clans, Irintsin, Khasakh, Barghutsin, Suisu up to Tungkin and Alair destroyed through fire all Ongghot figures, instruments and costumes of the shamans and shamanesses.'[12]

The persecution of shamanism among the Mongols, however, never rested on the private initiative of individual missionaries; it always went back to the Dalai Lama's command. The Third Dalai Lama first demanded the destruction of the Ongghot when he met with and converted Altan Khan in 1578. He imposed the same obligation on Abadai Khan of the Khalkha when Abadai requested

him to send missionaries to his subjects. Neyiči Toyin had his future
missionary activity in Eastern Mongolia prophesied by the Panchen
Lama at the end of his period of theological training,[13] and *Rab
'byams pa* Caya Pandita, the converter of North-West Mongolia,
received his mission in 1635 from the Fourth Dalai Lama: 'to go out
to the people of Mongolian language, to serve the faith and to show
men the teachings'.[14]

The Lamaist missionaries replaced the functions of the shamans
with similar practices from that area within Lamaism which consists
of a theological systematization of the old magical practices of
Indian and Tibetan folk religion, in other words from the realm of
Tantra. Already in India, Buddhism had been forced for the sake of
its diffusion and popularization to create the secret teaching of
Tantra, using and adopting very ancient popular magical practices.
Max Weber advanced a pertinent explanation for this development,
saying that it had to happen because 'the small urban householders
and peasants could hardly get very far with the products of the
soteriology of the educated aristocracy.'[15] In its struggle against the
local Tibetan *Bon* religion Buddhism in Tibet incorporated further
traits and deities from the *Bon po* demonology into its system. In the
confrontation between Lamaism and *Bon* the indigenous Tibetan
religion was forced by the more sophisticated, more highly developed
theological system, and also out of fear, to retreat and to camouflage
itself with Lamaist traits.[16] For its struggle against Mongolian
shamanism Lamaism thus had the example of the confrontation of
Buddhism with the *Bon* religion.

Tantrism, in the shape which it adopted as a substitute for the
shamanism prohibited among the Mongols, was applied, systematic
magic. Three Tantric methods offered parallels, and so substitutes,
for shamanism, and were therefore turned against it. These were the
use of exorcistic or protective formulae; the use of ritual gestures;
and the identification with a deity through a special form of
meditation.

The magical formulae (*dharani*) were taught to the Mongols by the
missionaries. It has already been indicated that their spread was
much promoted by donations from princes. Finds of excavations at
Olon Süme in Inner Mongolia bear witness to a preponderance of
short *dharani* intended to secure protection from demons and misfortune, and to obtain rebirth in the Buddhist paradise Sukhavati.
Among the earliest *dharani* formulae to be translated into Mongolian
are those to destroy evil, misfortune and demons, to protect and
increase cattle, keep away horse-plague, remove and dissolve
hindrances and 'drive out liver ailments'.[17] Neyiči Toyin propagated
especially the *dharani* of the system of Yamantaka and the *unio*

mystica, without giving any foundation for these. When a disciple once asked him why he taught these secret things to everyone, although he had nevertheless taught that they should not be accessible to anyone without initiation, Neyiči Toyin replied, 'You are perfectly right, but how can these simple people understand the deepest secrets, when one preaches to them just once? I am trying to gain their attention . . . .'[18] He succeeded in this with the aid of his method of distributing the exorcistic formulae to such a degree that around 1652 jealous clerics accused him of letting 'everyone recite Yamantaka prayers and other texts, starting from those who fetch water for the animals to drink, the collectors of cowdung and the gatherers of firewood, people who are unable to tell good from bad'.[19] Precisely in this way, however, he had won the common folk over to him, and when he died in 1653 he was praised above all by the 'simple folk, starting from those who fetch water for the animals to drink, the collectors of cowdung and the gatherers of firewood'.[20] The exorcistic and protective formulae provided by Lamaism in the form of *dharani* must have found an echo among the Mongols after shamanism had been persecuted and forbidden, for through them the individual could now operate directly. At the same time they made the shaman superfluous.

Much more significant yet, however, was the doctrine, anchored in the Tantra, of identification with a particular protective deity. Such a conception would be bound to be particularly familiar to the Mongols on account of the shamanist ideas concerning the guardian spirits of the ancestors, the Ongghot. To people who held that the mightiest shamans were those who ruled the most Ongghot, the vast pantheon of Lamaism, in which one god possessed many forms of manifestation, and in which fathers of the Church and local deities also took their place, must have seemed overwhelming.

Various types of Lamaist clergymen offered themselves to provide substitutes for the ecstatic functions of the shaman and for his exorcism. The *diyanči lama,* who cultivated meditation, enjoyed particular veneration here. To his normal novitiate and his theological education was added an especially difficult period of trial. Cut off from all profane things, he lived for 404 days in complete isolation and in prayer. This period fell into four equal periods, each of 101 days. During the first 101 days he prayed under a solitary tree on the edge of the steppe or the desert. Then followed 101 days of meditation at a spring, then 101 days of deep absorption on a mountain. The last and most difficult of the 101-day periods then had to be spent in prayer, fasting and deepest absorption on a place where corpses were exposed. The Mongols did not bury their dead, but exposed the corpses for wild animals to eat. During this last period of his trial the lama was forbidden to defend himself in any way against anything. Exhausted through the long fasting, and under the influence of his ritual precepts, the contemplative went through terrifying hallucinations and delusions. During this period, he also had to make his various ritual implements out of bones from the corpses; a rosary made out of human bones, a trumpet from a young girl's tibia and an eating-bowl from a human skull. Often he also made a double drum (Skt. *damaru*) out of two skull-caps with skin stretched over them.[21] After these trials such a *diyanči lama* lived as a respected magician and hermit. A further, more elevated form of substitute for the exorcizing shaman was provided by the *gurtum* (Tib. *sku rten*) *lama*. This name was given to a lama who possessed the ability of placing himself into ecstasy and trance in order to drive out demons and ask questions concerning the future. These sooth-sayer- and magician-lamas mostly lived in monasteries, which enjoyed special fame through their presence. This led to an increase in the influx of believers. The *gurtum lama* was invited to come and display his art at all great temple festivals, at the religious masked dances (*čam* = Tib. *'cham*) at the beginning and middle of the year, at the fire-offerings of many rich families in the ninth or twelfth months of the year. According to the Mongolian conception, the *gurtum lama* was a magical, mysterious and feared person who was connected with the fierce deities, and who in the state of ecstasy was himself one of their forms of manifestation. F. D. Lessing noted down in the 1930s a very interesting characterization of the *gurtum* by a Mongolian lama. Asked whether the *gurtum lama* then was not a shaman, the lama replied: 'Far from it, he is much higher. He invokes the proper spirits, not the impure ones of the shaman.'[22] This appreciation shows clearly that we are concerned with the same ideas as with the ecstatic shaman, and portrays the *gurtum* as the adaptation of these ideas within the Lamaist doctrinal structure. The Lamaist prototype for the *gurtum* was certainly provided by the Lamaist state oracle of the *Chos skyong* in Lhasa, who went into ecstasy and trance several times each year with reference to affairs of major importance. It is not clear whether ecstasy and trance were produced merely through self-hypnosis or through the use of intoxicating means also. The physical powers manifested on this occasion are supranormal; thus a *Chos skyong* oracle priest in Tibet wore without assistance from others an iron hat which normally could not be held by several men.[23] Similar cases of exceptional physical achievements are also found amongst shamans. Japanese scholars report a 76-year old shamaness, who on her own account already had to spend all day in bed from the weakness of age, but who during her exorcistic activity would exorcize in ecstasy through a whole night in heavy ceremonial clothes without exhaustion.

The *gurtum* wears an upper garment of silk over a piece of clothing like a woman's skirt of blue cotton. The lower part of this garment is decorated with skulls; according to his own explanation, these are the same emblems as those of the terrifying deities. The apron changes him into a Bodhisattva. This is in principle the same idea as with the shaman, only edged with Buddhist concepts. Also among the *gurtum*'s clothing is a collar, which in Buddhist iconography is equally reserved for Bodhisattvas. Over the collar he wears, however, a typical shamanist emblem, namely a silver mirror. Without doubt the connection with the Tantric doctrinal structure is again visible here, for in the middle of this mirror is always found a mystical syllable, out of which the deity is manifested in meditation and evocation. Five flags decorate the back, and are fastened to a special belt around the hips. They resemble those flags that Chinese actors often use. On the head a large helmet is worn, decorated with skulls; it is bound firmly under the mouth with strips of *khatag* to prevent the *gurtum* from biting off his tongue in ecstasy. The flags, according to the *gurtum*'s explanations, have the same significance as the Ongghot for the shaman; they incorporate, that is, the powers which fight against the evil demons. Here we are speaking of the evil demons of the unbelievers, again a theological refinement. At the beginning of the ceremony the *gurtum* holds the thunderbolt-symbol and the magic dagger (*phur bu*) in his hands. Then his disciples read the ritual prescription for the god concerned. When the moment of identification with the deity arrives, the *gurtum* is possessed by this protective spirit, who is classified in Lamaist iconography as a *dharmapala* (Tib. *chos skyong*), a guardian of the Law. Then he grasps a sword, blood-like foam comes from his mouth, his whole body trembles and he strikes about him wildly with the sword; in other words, the protective spirit of the Lamaist church which has entered him fights against the demon. In this state of ecstasy he can also make predictions. The Mongols come one after another, present him with offering scarves and ask about illnesses, business prospects and so on. The answers are given in an unknown speech, which one of the *gurtum*'s assistants translates.

H. Hoffmann has said of the Tibetan state oracle of the *chos skyong*, the Lamaist prototype of the *gurtum*, that it is a living relic of the *Bon* religion in Lamaism, and indeed of that side of *Bon* which stands close to the shamanism of the Siberian peoples.[24] With the progress of Lamaism in Mongolia, however, one can observe more and more such parallel phenomena to the *chos skyong* oracle of Lhasa as substitutes for the shamanism which had been driven out and outlawed. Such 'sword-shamans', as they are also known on account of their ecstatic striking about with swords, are equally known among the half-Mongolian Tujen on the Kokonor region.[25] The occurrence of *gurtum* has frequently been reported for the Mongols. From Eastern Mongolia there is, in addition, a weakened form of the *gurtum*, the so-called *layĭcing*, who also acts as a shaman-substitute. *Layĭcing* could be a deformation of the Tibetan name *gNas chung*, referring to the state oracle. The *layĭcing* does not belong to a religious community; he is a layman. During his conjuration he wears a coat of mail and a helmet, which are at other times kept in the temple, and in place of the shaman's drum he strikes cymbals taken from the instruments used in Lamaist temple music. During the conjuration he reads Lamaist prayers, through the aid of which he is to become the master of the demons of illness. There are both male and female *layĭcing*. *Layĭcing* were observed in East Mongolia as late as 1942/3.[26] The *layĭcing* can be regarded as a transitional form to the Lamaist version of shamanism, from the time when Lamaism came to tolerate shamanism once more. This evolution from *gurtum* to *layĭcing* shows unambiguously, however, that Lamaism at first consciously introduced the ecstatic form of the Tibetan state oracle, taken over from pre-Buddhist *Bon*, into Mongolia as the *gurtum* to provide a substitute for the suppressed shaman.

Indications are lacking in our sources of whether the Lamaist church, in the more than three hundred years which have passed since the beginning of its persecution of shamanism, has ever altogether succeeded in suppressing this local Mongolian religious form entirely. The development seen as a whole speaks against it. Flexible in its defence, shamanism began to camouflage itself through accepting Buddhist phrases and through invoking Buddhist divinities conjointly, until in the course of time it appeared acceptable to the Lamaist church.

On the Lamaist side strong syncretistic tendencies were observable from the outset. These tendencies had the object of accepting and systematizing the local gods of Mongolian folk religion in a manner analogous to the prototype of the Lamaist incorporation of characteristic traits and deities from the Tibetan *Bon* religion.

The first Peking *lCang skya* Khutukhtu, *Ngag dbang blo bzang chos ldan* (1642–1714), had already inserted the protective gods of Činggis Khan into the Lamaist pantheon, in writing a prayer for the worship of Činggis Khan which had been requested by members of the Mongolian aristocracy.[27] His personal disciple, *sMon lam rab 'byams pa bsTan 'dzin grags pa* of Ujumchin, attempted again to incorporate the making of an incense-offering to drive away evil into a prayer, in which he sought to include in the Lamaist pantheon the animal-headed protective deities of Mongolia, concerning whom the

Third Dalai Lama spoke for the first time in 1578 on his journey to Altan Khan.[28] The Mergen Diyanči *bla ma-yin Blo bzang bstan pa'i rgyal mtshan*, a Lamaist clergyman from the South Mongolian region of Urat, living in the middle of the eighteenth century, distinguished himself particularly in the formation of prayers which united in a syncretic manner ideas and deities of shamanism with Lamaist ritual forms. He created prayers for the cult of high places, for the fire-offering, the consecration of houses and so on, in which he provided fragments of old prayers of the folk religion with Lamaist formulae, changed their deities, and incorporated them into the total liturgical structure of Lamaism.[29] His attempts to produce such a new liturgy were in part so successful (they were distributed through blockprints) that many of his syncretistic prayers were transmitted anonymously as folk-religious prayers, and were mixed with other old prayers from the folk religion.[30] The second *lCang skya* khutukhtu, *Rol pa'i rdo rje* (1717–86), also moved in this direction, in seeking to unite in one prayer Geser Khan and the Chinese war-god Kuan-ti,[31] and at the end of the nineteenth century a prayer to the Lords of the Earth composed by a North Mongolian lama was still being distributed as a blockprint.[32] All these productions fitted in with the tendency of shamanism to camouflage itself with Lamaist emblems and formulae. The Lamaist church took part itself in this fusion of Lamaist and shamanist concepts and ideas, which now became reflected in expressions of the folk religion. A legend from the East Mongolian Küriye banner, which was still being told in 1943, illustrates what the relation between Lamaism and shamanism finally became. At the time when the Küriye banner was founded (sixteenth century) the Lama doctrine flourished very much; the shamanist religion brought by immigrants was on the other hand discredited and suppressed. Thus the two kinds of religion, the yellow and the black, were hostile to each other through a long period of time. Later, about a hundred years ago, a very skilled shaman said, 'I will take revenge on the Lamas.' One night he sent the Ongghot to the leader of the Lamas, the brain of this lama was struck by sickness and it is said that he could not move his body at all. Thus it later came about that the two religions now tolerated each other and no longer fought each other.[33]

If there thus came about in the course of time a toleration on the part of Lamaism, and a peaceful co-existence of shamanism and Lamaism, in our century persecutions of shamanism by the state have begun. The legislation of the Mongolian People's Republic makes shamanist activity liable to punishment, as a consequence indeed of the generally anti-religious attitude of Communist states. In the Eastern and Southern Mongol territories of China shamanism was still a practised religion, against which nothing was undertaken officially, at the time of Japanese influence over these territories. Attempts were nevertheless made through the newspapers and such of Inner Mongolia to discredit the shamans and their supposed successes in healing and to make them laughable, through caricatures in comic-strip style. Thus one of these anti-shamanist picture-strips shows how the shaman is called to a sick person. When the sick father dies during the shaman's invocations, the indignant son shows the shaman the door. As a crowning misfortune the shaman's horse bolts, he falls in a river and suffers all kinds of injury. In this way his powerlessness, and the imposture of his activity, is portrayed. To this the recommendation is added that in cases of illness one should call a doctor rather than a shaman.

If Buddhism in present-day Mongolia has completely lost its influence, shamanism despite all its persecutions continues as a form of religion. Incantations of pure, mixed and completely Lamaized forms can be recorded by field research in all parts of Mongolia up to the present day. In one East Mongolian region, where in the 1940s up to thirty shamans and shamanesses could still be counted, shamanism was still in full swing in 1951.[34] In 1960 songs of shamans were still being noted down in Northern Mongolia, in the Bargha territory and in Southern Mongolia.[35]

FIVE

THE MONGOLIAN FOLK RELIGION AND ITS PANTHEON

Alongside the rituals and songs of conjuration (*daγudalγa*) of ecstatic shamanism there are many other forms of expression of a Mongolian folk religion, in the prayers to Eternal Blue Heaven (Köke Mongke Tngri), in the fire-prayers, the worship of Činggis Khan as ancestral lord of the families of princely origin, the invocations to gods in the form of armoured men on horseback (such as Sülde Tngri, Dayičin Tngri and Geser Khan), the prayers to the White Old Man (Čaγan Ebügen) and to the constellation of the Great Bear (Doluγan Ebügen) and in the prayers of the cult of high places. These various kinds of folk-religious prayers, as they can be characterized in opposition to the expressions of pure, mixed and Lamaized shamanism, present extensive points of agreement and similarities in expression which point back to the original presence of extremely old prototypes which shine through all the trimmings of later periods, alterations, reworkings and cases of camouflage through the adoption of Lamaist phrases and forms.[1]

The rituals of the folk religion were performed by laymen, by members of the family concerned or by a lay speaker (*gara baγsi*), without the participation of either shamans or, later, of Lamaist monks.

The most widespread form in which this folk religion appears is the incense-offering (*sang* or *ubsang* = Tibetan *bsangs*), in which juniper branches (*arča*) were originally burnt, although incense (*küji*) is more common. There are incense offerings for all possible occasions and to each of the various deities: to the White Old Man, to Geser Khan, Činggis Khan, the mountain gods, the wind-horse flag and so on.[2]

The fire-prayers are recited at sacrificial ceremonies (*takilγa*) at which offerings such as the breast-bone of a sheep, covered with coloured ribbons and melted butter, are burnt. In parts of Mongolia, especially in the north, the fire-offering is celebrated exclusively by women, on the twenty-ninth day of the last month of the year,[3] while in the East Mongolian regions the fire-offering can be performed only by the master of the house or his sons.[4]

Apart from the fire-prayer proper (öcig), the ceremony of invitation (dalalγa) forms a significant part of the fire-cult. This dalalγa-ceremony is also attached to many other offering-prayers of the Mongols, and names the principal gods. During the naming and invocation of the various gods and the making of requests to them, the deity and the things desired are shown the direction to the worshippers through an arrow, to the shaft of which are attached gold, pearls, little pieces of silver, silk strips and cereal grains; those present accompany this with the cry qurui, qurui.[5]

The benedictions (irügel) which are recited on all important occasions in life, such as marriage, birth, departure for hunting or travel, construction of a new tent or house, selection of foals, rounding up of herds and so on, as well as the blessings in connection with the anointing (miliyal) of the newly-born, of animals, clothes, tools, tents and houses, and weapons, and also the praises (maγtaγal) all have religious significance, as too do imprecations and curses (qariyal);[6] in all these the magical power of the spoken word is of particular significance.

The daily necessities and activities of life, and the festivals connected with the end of the year and with aspects of the economic life such as the raising of animals, hunting and primitive agriculture, have not yet lost their relationship to the religious; connections exist everywhere.

An analysis of the numerous prayers from this domain provides information about the rich world of gods of Mongolian folk religion.

1 Eternal Heaven

The constant use of the Mongolian expression möngke tngri-yin kücündür, 'through the power of Eternal Heaven', in epistles, ordinances, order tablets (p'ai-tzu) and stone inscriptions of the Mongol dynasty (thirteenth to fourteenth centuries)[7] bears witness to the belief of the Mongols in the presence of a heavenly power to which all powers of and above the earth are subject. The oldest Mongolian historical source, the Secret History of the Mongols, a work of the thirteenth century, also mentions prayer to Eternal Heaven, and offerings fixed on poles and strewn about which were made to the sun which represented it.[8] Činggis Khan received his mission from Mighty Heaven: 'I was designated by Mighty Heaven';[9] Heaven gives the realm to him. He says, 'If Heaven will truly give the realm into my power . . .'.[10] These references confirm the reports of European travellers and missionaries of the thirteenth century concerning a belief in a High God among the Mongols: 'they believe in one god, of whom they believe that he is the creator of all visible and invisible things . . .', wrote John of Plano Carpini.[11] Tngri, Eternal Heaven (Möngke Tngri) or Mighty Heaven (Erketü Tngri) is the supreme god of heaven. In the Cumanian psalms of Mary, *tngri* unequivocally translates Deus.[12] The *Yüan-shih*, chapter 77, describes a Mongolian sacrifice called 'sprinkling with mare's milk' in which a horse, eight wethers and other items are sacrificed to heaven, and Činggis Khan is invoked.[13]

This conception has also been preserved to later times in the folk religion. Köke Möngke Tngri, 'Blue Eternal Heaven' is 'the highest of all the heavenly beings [*tngri*]';[14] he is also called 'Khan Eternal Heaven',[15] the 'Supreme Lord of Everything'.[16] He has special prayers of his own, but he is also mentioned in many other religious ceremonies and customs.

Köke Möngke Tngri dwells in the sky: 'Above is my Blue Eternal Heaven, below is my Mother Earth.'[17] He created all things.[18] The life-supporting fire 'arose through the prior decision [*ǰaγaγa*] of Blue Eternal Heaven',[19] livestock were born according to his decision and foresight: 'The milk of your blue-spotted mare, who was born according to a decision coming down from the Eternal Lord of Heaven' comes from an invocation for the libation on the occasion of consecrating mares.[20] The Black Sülde standard of Činggis Khan is referred to in the prayers directed to it as 'planted and erected by Blue Eternal Heaven'.[21]

Sun and moon are subject to him.[22] He is the Father of Heaven (*tenggeri ečige*),[23] and as such one calls on him for protection and help:

Father of Heaven, sacrificing I pray to you,
you who protect my body,
who take illness and sorrow away from me,
who keep far from me the danger of the knife.
Father of Heaven, sacrificing I pray to you,
you who defeat brigands and bandits,
those who act covetously,
you who keep far from me the danger of the evil devil . . ..[24]

One appeals to him in order to obtain fortune and happiness for one's sons and daughters.[25] In the request formulae which are attached to most fire-hymns[26] one requests 'the blessing of the Father, of Eternal Heaven';[27] at the consecration of a newly-erected yurt one asks, 'May Khan Möngke Tngri live and rule at your left hand';[28] and at the libations of blessing the foals on the occasion of the sorting out of foals in summer the nine times nine libations to Khan Möngke Tngri take first place.[29]

2 The heavenly beings (*tngri*)

Over and over again in the folk-religious prayers and the shamans' songs of conjuration it is stated that there is a total number of ninety-nine *tngri* (heavenly beings). They say 'Above are the ninety-nine *tngri* . . . below the seventy-seven levels of Mother Earth.'[30] There chief is Köke Möngke Tngri, 'Eternal Blue Heaven'. Often, too, the texts speak of 'the ninety-nine eternal heaven-gods [*möngke tngri*] above'.[31]

The ninety-nine *tngri* form a dualistic scheme along with the Earth-Mother, Etügen Eke. Often she too is spoken of as consisting of seventy-seven earth-mothers[32]—the *itoga* of Plano Carpini[33] and the *natigai* or *nacigai* of Marco Polo's account.[34]

According to the shamans' version the ninety-nine *tngri* fall into two groups, as is shown by their songs and by the prayers of the Mongolian folk religion:

> My forty-four *tngri* of the eastern side,
> my fifty-five *tngri* of the western side,
> my three *tngri* of the northern side . . .[35]

With the three gods of the North a total of 102 *tngri* is reached.

A nineteenth-century Buryat Mongol description of Mongolian shamanism explains

that there are fifty-five supreme *tngri* in the West, forty-four in the East, altogether ninety-nine *tngri*. Of the fifty-five *tngri* of the West fifty are worshipped through prayer and five through sacrifices . . . of the forty-four *tngri* of the East forty are worshipped through prayer and four through sacrifices . . . .[36]

Alongside the idea of ninety-nine gods (*tngri*) there is also a conception of a group of thirty-three gods, whose chief is Qormusta. He is called 'Qormusta, King of the *tngri*',[37] also 'King Qormusta'.[38] D. Banzarov had already supposed that this was an adaptation of the Iranian Ahuramazda.[39] An influence from Indian concepts of Indra with the thirty-three planets is equally easy to imagine. In fact, Qormusta Tngri is also equated with Esrua (= Brahma).[40] At what time the infiltration of this Iranian divine figure took place, and above all by what route, at present still remains to be explained. At any rate a collection of *mantras* and *dharanis* in four languages which was printed in 1431 already mentions *qormusta qan tngri*,

'Qormusta King of the Gods'.[41] However, Qormusta Tngri is not only named as chief of the thirty-three gods, but also as supreme head of all of the ninety-nine *tngri* of the Mongols: 'the ninety-nine *tngri* with Qormusta at their head'[42] are spoken of, and 'the ninety-nine *tngri* commanded by Qormusta the King of the Gods'.[43] In a collection of Mongolian proverbial wisdom, which may have been made before the sixteenth century, the proverb occurs:

> The highest of the gods [*tngri*] is Möngke Tngri [Eternal Heaven], Their king is Qormusta Tngri . . . .[44]

In addition to his function as ruler of the heavenly beings, Qormusta Tngri also stands in special connection with the origin of fire. Many of the Mongol fire-hymns say that Buddha struck the light and 'Qormusta Tngri lit the fire'.[45]

The *tngri* also often come in specific groups of gods formed according to number, such as the gods of the four corners (*dörben jobkis-un tngri*), the five gods of the winds (*kei-yin tabun tngri*), the five gods of the entrance (*egüden-u tabun tngri*),[46] the four Tüsid Tngri,[47] five Lightning Tngri (*čakilyan-u tabun tngri*), the five gods of the door (*quyalyan-u tabun tngri*), the five gods of the horizontal (*köndüleng-un 5 tngri*), the five Qadaraya Tngri,[48] the seven Your Tngri[49] and the seven Kötegci Tngri, the seven Steam Tngri (*ayur-un 7 tngri*) and the seven Thunder Gods (*ayungyui-yin 7 tngri*), [50] the Gods of the Eight Borders (*nayiman kijayar-un tngri*),[51] the Nine Gods of Anger (*kiling-ün 9 tngri*), the Nine Iruči Tngri and the Nine Yellow Gods (*sirabur 9 tngri*).[52]

The request for a comprehensive enumeration and description of all the *tngri* in the Mongolian pantheon was advanced as early as 1846, by Dorji Banzarov in his study of Mongolian popular religion;[53] at the same time he indicated the almost insuperable difficulties which stand in the way of such a project. These obstacles have not become much less today, even if the amount of source-material for the task, in the form of prayers, shamanistic hymns and folklore texts, which is available has been multiplied many times. What exists, however, provides no definitive picture, and new materials are constantly being uncovered. Nevertheless the sources known today allow one to assemble a large number of names of *tngri*. For some of these it is possible to indicate particular functions and even iconographical details.

Tngri mentioned in the Mongolian prayers and hymns, blessing and consecration formulae include, apart from those already mentioned, the following:

Ajirai Tngri
Aqa Tngri ('Elder Brother Tngri')

Aryasar Arači Tngri
Arsi Tngri ('Hermit Tngri')
Aruči Tngri
Anarba Tngri
Ataya Tngri
Bayatur Tngri ('Tngri of Heroes')
Bayatur Čayan Tngri
Bayan Čayan Tngri ('Tngri of White Riches')
Barayun Tngri ('West God')
Bisman Tngri
Bisiiči Tngri (= Bayasuyčid Tngri)
Bisnu Tngri
Boquma Tngri
Burqan Tngri
Čayan Ebügen Tngri ('White Old Man Tngri')
Dayisun Tngri ('Enemy God')
Degedü Tngri ('Supreme God')
Degere Tngri ('Sublime God')
Degüü Tngri ('Younger Brother Tngri')
Düsid (Tüsid)-ün Tngri
Eberen Tngri
Egüden Yeke Tngri ('Great God of the Door')
Elbesküi Tngri
El Lan Yeke Tngri
Ejen Tngri ('Ruler Tngri')
Egüle-yin Kölügelegči Tngri ('Tngri Riding on the Clouds')
Edürün Ergegči Tngri
Erenggüngge Tngri
Erketü Tngri ('Mighty Tngri')
Esrün Tngri ('Esru-a Tngri')
Gölüger Tngri
Güjir Küngkür Tngri (= Maqagala Darqan Güjir Tngri)
Гajar Delekei Tngri Ejed
Гal-un Ökin Tngri ('Fire Devi Tngri')
Гal Tngri ('Fire Tngri')
Гodoli Ulayan Tngri ('Red Arrow Tngri')
Jaryuči Tngri
Jayayayači Tngri ('Fate Tngri')
Jil-ün Tngri ('Year Tngri')
Jirüken Qara Tngri
Jol Tngri (= Jol Nemegülegči Tngri)
Kesig-ün Tngri ('Fortune Tngri')
Keter Doysin Tngri
Kisaya Tngri

Kököge Sibaγun Tngri ('Cuckoo Tngri')
Kölčin Tngri
Küler Tngri
Manaqan Tngri
Mal-un Tngri ('Cattle Tngri')
Miliyan Tngri ('Tngri of Anointing')
Nereči Tngri
Ningbudava Tngri
Nomči Tngri
Noyan Babai Tngri
Odutan Tngri
Öbsečer (Ebügejer) Jol Tngri
Öggügsen Tngri
Ökin Tngri ('Maiden Tngri')
Ömči Tngri
Öndegen Tngri ('Eggs Tngri')
Qadarγa Buum Tngri
Qan Güjir Tngri
Qan Tngri ('Prince Tngri')
Qayiruγ-i Ürečigülügči Tngri
Očirwani Tngri
Qura Baγulγaγči Tngri ('Tngri who makes the rain fall')
Qotqui Ulaγan Tngri
Quular Tngri
Oyur Qara Noyan Tngri
Odqon Qara Tngri ('Black Youngest-born Tngri')
Siremel Ökin Tngri ('Bronze Heavenly Fairy Tngri')
Suu Tngri ('Majesty Tngri')
Sülde Tngri
Teken Tngri ('Billygoat Tngri')
Tariyan-i Arbidqaγči Tngri ('Tngri who increases the fruits of the field')
Talbiγči Tngri
Yeke Suu Jali Tngri ('Tngri of Great Majesty and Glory')
Yeke Sudtu Mangγus Tngri
Učiral Tngri

Doubtless further names could be found which would bring the total number to more than ninety-nine *tngri*. In doing so one would find strong local differences, as a result of the acceptance of local gods. In addition, late adoptions from the Buddhist pantheon include Bisman Tngri (= Vaisravana), Bisnu Tngri (= Visnu), Burqan Tngri (= Buddha), Esrün Tngri (= Indra), Ökin Tngri (= Sridevi) and Očirwani Tngri (= Vajrapani). Nine out of the large number of *tngri* are often named. The grouping of the 'Nine Great Tngri' in the prayers is not however always the same.[54] Möngke Tngri (Eternal Heaven) and Qormusta Tngri are always included among them. The attributes and iconography of the various *tngri*, in so far as one can deduce it from the various prayers, makes it appear that the *tngri*, the gods or heavenly beings, have primarily a protective function. This is particularly clear with reference to Bayatur Tngri, 'Tngri of Heroes':

Created by the Holy Master Buddha,
Appealed to by Qormusta Tngri . . .
At the front door . . .
On the green steppe,
on the ravendark-grey horse,
with a sword of hard steel.
You who give the best of the countries . . .
Supreme Khan over all, Tngri of Heroes . . .
With your great, tall jasper body,
With your pure, high voice, you who
Like a support of elm-wood
Hold me up in the ribs,
When I slip,
You who like a support of larch-wood
Hold me up in the ribs
When I lose my footing, my *tngri*,
You who change my clothing into armour and helmet
And into a winter coat of kid-skin,
My *tngri* . . .[55]

Kisaya Tngri, also called Kihanya Tngri[56] or Ulayan Kihang, 'Red Kisang Tngri'[57] among the Buryats, lives in the north-west and rides a horse of isabelline (greyish-yellow) colour, with brown eyes. He counts as the protector of riches and of the souls of living beings.

I pray and bow down to the mighty Khan, Kisaya Tngri,
Who has a great jasper body,
Who has a harmonious, clear voice,
Who does not let the approaching arrow strike,
Who is a protective wall if I fall,
Who makes my clothing into armour and helmet,
Who makes my life in this world eternal and assured . . ..[58]

Qan Kisaya Tngri also has the same epithets of supporter and protector as Bayatur Tngri, 'you who support me in the ribs like a support of elm'.[59] He lives in the west.[60]

Ataγa Tngri, who has a series of functions closely resembling those of Eternal Heaven, counts as the protector of horses, especially among the Aga and Khori Buryats.[61] He is also referred to as Red Ataγa Tngri.[62] He and the other *tngri* are sacrificed to in connection with the well-being of herds of cattle too.[63]

> . . . Khan Ataγa Tngri,
> Your thundering voice
> Is heard close to the abyss,
> Unifier of the thoughts of the Mongols . . .
> With gigantic, great body like lightning,
> Ruler over many clouds,
> With ten thousand eyes,
> My Ataγa Tngri, supreme over all, . . .
> My *tngri*, who clothes my naked body,
> My *tngri*, who gives food for my mouth to eat,
> My *tngri*, who gives me clothes to put on my back,
> My *tngri*, who gives me a mount to ride with my thighs,
> My *tngri*, who keeps far away the messengers of the God of
>   Death (Erlig Khan) who come to take me away and destroy me,
> May you grant me the blessing and good fortune of your
>   protection . . . .[64]

Jayaγayči Tngri, the 'Tngri of Fate', is a bringer of good fortune and blessings, and above all protects herds and property. As 'Star of Fate Tngri' (Odun Jayaγayči Tngri) he dwells at the zenith,[65] but he was created in the South, and created out of himself, not by almighty Eternal Heaven.[66] This primogeniture is always emphasized as a special quality,[67] although he is also called he who 'is prayed to by Qormusta and brought forth by the Holy Master Buddha';[68] this attests a more recent Buddhist influence on this divine figure from the folk religion. He is entitled to his own incense-offering prayers,[69] and received as offerings a white horse, a white sheep, nine coloured pieces of cloth, nine lamps, nine incense-sticks and libations.[70] A libation-prayer for the well-being of cattle calls him 'God of Fate of the many multi-coloured, spotted cows, and of those with a white spot who belong to the Mongolian sovereign';[71] he also appears in a blessing for foals.[72] His blessing is requested 'coming from the East' for the newly-constructed tent,[73] similarly he is asked to protect the horse's harness and its accessories,[74] to give food, a horse, and long life, and to save from devils (*čidkür*) and evil spirits (*ada*). Above all, however, he is asked to preserve one from injury, especially from becoming crippled, and to look after the well-being of parents, wife and children.[75] He lets the herd-animals 'grow great without illness'[76] Often Jayaγači Tngri is invoked as 'bringer of fate, god of good fortune (kesig)'.[77]

The functions of certain of the heavenly beings (tngri) closely resemble those of the supreme god of heaven, Khan Möngke Tngri or 'Eternal Heaven'. Erketü Tngri, 'the Mighty Tngri' or 'Mighty Heaven', is also referred to as 'self-created'[78] and bears explicit traits of a creator-god. He called Yesügei, father of Činggis Khan, into being;[79] both the Mother of Fire, El Γalaqan Eke, and the 'Fire-Herd of the Sovereign'[80] owe their origin to him;[81] the 'great White Sülde [standard] of the Emperor arose through the decision [jayaγa] of Erketü Tngri',[82] and even the 'imperial daughters-in-law were . . . born through the decision of Erketü Tngri'.[83] Erketü Tngri thus takes on the appearance of a creator-god with a special relationship to the imperial house of the Činggisids.

Degere Tngri, 'Sublime Heaven', who is often called upon, possesses a similar creator-role, as does Miliyan Tngri,[84] who corresponds to Esege Malan Tngri (conceived of as the supreme god, analogous to 'Eternal Heaven') among the Buryats.[85] He is omniscient and bears the epithets 'Miliyan Tngri, the Mighty [erketü], whose knowledge is overflowing'[86] and 'Miliyan Tngri who knows all things'.[87]

The figures of Eternal (Blue) Heaven (Köke Möngke Tngri), Ataγa Tngri, Baγatur Tngri, Erketü Tngri, Degere Tngri and Miliyan Tngri cannot be very clearly separated from each other.[88]

As their name already indicates, some tngri are explicitly gods of riches and fertility: Elbesküi Tngri, 'Increaser Tngri', who is called upon for the increase of property;[89] Öggügči or Öggügsen Tngri, 'Giver Tngri',[90] and Jol Nemegülügči Tngri, 'Increaser of Good Fortune Tngri'.[91]

The heavenly beings stand in close relationship with the principal economic activities of the Mongols, especially the breeding of herds. They are however, as with the creator-gods and gods of prosperity, not simply concerned with the protection and increase of the herds in general; certain among them, rather, each have a favourable influence on specific kinds of animal and specific aspects of Mongolian animal-raising.

Thus Ningbudaya Tngri is the god who 'lets the yak herds become numerous'; he is 'a tngri who multiplies the yak-cows [qayinuγ]' and one who 'increases the baliyama cattle'. Suu Tngri, 'Genius Tngri', is the 'increaser of the many red cattle of Nepal' while Erenggüngge Tngri is 'increaser of the many maki-cattle of India' and Jarluγ Sangbuu-a Tngri is 'increaser of the many brown-red cattle of Tibet'. Quudan Wang Tngri aids the growth of the 'fruits of the earth and the many spotted cattle of the Chinese

T'ai-ping Emperor' while Teken Tngri, 'Billygoat Tngri', influences the increase of the 'long-horned blue cows' of the Maĵaris and Ĵol Tngri aids the growth of the 'red-blue spotted cows of the black Chinese'.[92]

Red Ataɣa Tngri (Ata Tngri?) is an especial dispenser of fortune for horses, while Red Godoli Tngri assures the fortune of cows.[93]

Güjir Küngker Tngri gives sufficient fodder for the herds and enough food for men.[94] With the Lamaist title of Mahakala he appears among the Buryats as Maqa Galan Darqan Güjir Tngri, 'Mahakala Smith Güjir Tngri', and is a special protective god of horned cattle.[95]

> Great Maqa Galan Darqan Güjir Tngri,
> Eldest brother of the ninety-nine *tngri,*
> Who arose through the blessing of Qormusta Tngri
> At the command of the holy Teacher Buddha,
> You who have a glorious cast-iron shield,
> You who have a beautiful coloured throne,
> You who have a great golden hammer,
> You who have a great silver anvil,
> You, Maqa Galan Darqan Güjir Tngri, I worship,
> Deign to come here on your blue-grey horse . . .
> You who determine all things,
> Deign to come here on a black horse, . . .
> For the sake of my son's life and soul . . .
> For the sake of the life and soul of the four kinds of livestock,
> That live in the steppe, I ask you[96]

Manaqan Tngri on the other hand is the god of hunting:

> Čoo, čoo, Manaqan with a body of crude silver,
> Khan Manaqan, with tens of thousands of wild animals in
>   his power,
> Čoo, čoo, Khan Manaqan with a body of gold and silver,
> Khan Manaqan, with the wild animals in his power,
> Khan Manaqan the mighty, who gives without error,
> Khan Manaqan, who gives without pity . . . .[97]

Manaqan Tngri is the lord of all the 'thousands upon thousands of game-animals';[98] he is implored for a rich catch:

> I ask, let all those who are mine have food to eat . . .
> I ask, let all the people have food . . .
> I ask, appoint food for all . . . .[99]

He bestows good fortune in hunting on the steppes and in the mountains, he makes the eye sharp and steadies the hunter's hand.

> Make my hand steady when shooting,
> Make my eye sharp when on the look-out . . . .[100]

Alongside the general god of hunting, Manaqan Tngri, there are also local hunting-spirits, such as the hunting Ongghon Bayanmani among the Ordos,[101] or the Buryat hunter-Ongghon, Anda Bars,[102] which have ceremonies (*dalalγa*) of their own dedicated to them.

The growth of the fruits of the field also stands under a particular *tngri*, Tariyan-i Arbidqaγči Tngri, 'Tngri who Increases the Fruits of the Field'.[103]

Wind, thunder, clouds of mist, lightning and clouds have their own groups of *tngri*.[104] In the South-West resides the White Lightning-Tngri, riding on a white horse, along with his companions the seventy-seven *siqar*, the ninety-nine Rumblers (*kükür*) and the thirteen terrible thunder-*tngri*.[105] Rain is subject to Qura Baγulγaγči Tngri, 'Tngri who Lets the Rain Fall'.[106]

Some of the Heavenly Ones are called upon for quite specific things, for example Bisman Tngri, who besides the increase of possessions also bestows the strengthening of bodily powers,[107] Visiiči Tngri, called on for respect from everybody,[108] Kölčin Tngri for freeing from and protection from boils, scabs, vermin and worms,[109] Anarba Tngri for beauty,[110] Bayan Caγan Tngri, 'White Riches Tngri, who lives in the South-West' against accident and infection,[111] Qon Baγatur Tngri, who lives in the North-West, for the removal of injuries in exchange for a substitute-image,[112] the Heavenly Maiden Tngri (Siremel or Sirmaγ Ökin Tngri),[113] who rides on a yellow goat or on yellow clouds, against grief and against demons, Boquma Tngri, 'Bubonic Plague Tngri', against bubonic plague,[114] Keter Doγsin Tngri, the 'violent Tngri who looks for fights', as 'lord of trials and contests' and Qadarγa Buum Tngri as 'Lord of Curses'.[115] Other *tngri* such as Öbegejir Tngri, Elder Brother Tngri (Aqa Tngri) and Younger Brother Tngri (Degüü Tngri)[116] and many other heavenly beings are called upon without specification of their tasks and functions. In connection with many of the heavenly beings iconographic indications are given, as is shown by the examples given above (Baγatur Tngri, Kisaγa Tngri, Ataγa Tngri, Güjir Küngker Tngri, Manaqan Tngri and Siremel Ökin Tngri). These are however mostly restricted to the colour of the body and that of the animal on which the god rides. Some of the shamans' songs of invocation contain more detailed information on the appearance of the *tngri* being called upon,[117] who is almost always a local deity. Thus for example the following is said by a Bulgan shaman about Noyan Babai Tngri:

> You who come and make

The white Garuda-bird
Tremble in its multiplicity of colour, A hui.
You who dwell in the tops of the pines,
You who have whorls of hair as big as a man's chest,
You who have nine times nine, eighty-one, whorls of hair,
Noyan Babai Tngri,
All of the Noyan Babai Tngri, You
Who have your seat on this side of rTa mgrin [Skt. Hayagrīva],
   the Lord of the Law,
I invite you, I ask you to come . . . .[118]

Qan Güjir Tngri, 'Prince Güjir Tngri', is described in the following way in an invocation to a local mountain god:

My prince Güjir Tngri,
You who eat burning fire,
You who have a fiery serpent for your staff,
A rage-maddened wolf for your mount,
Human flesh as food,
Bronze and stone for heart,
You who slink up like the crouching wolf,
You who tear like the grasping wolf . . . .[119]

On the other hand Kököge Sibaγun Tngri, the 'Cuckoo Tngri', is described like this:

Kököge Sibaγun Tngri,
Who sets out towards the thirteen Altai [mountains]
Looking out as he goes,
Who goes towards the twenty-two Köküi [mountains],
To spend one or two nights there
With the thick tree as dwelling,
With the slender tree as seat . . . .[120]

The names of the tngri are frequently changed by numerous additional epithets. Thus in the songs of the Buryat shamans more than eight names occur for Noyan Babai Tngri,[121] and in a shaman's song noted down in 1960 from the Old Bargha banner the complex of names Yisün Sülde Ataγa Buumal Tngri, 'Nine Sülde Ataγa The Descender Tngri', is found as a name for Ataγa Tngri.[122]

Many of the tngri are linked to particular regions of the world, in other words they are thought of as living in a particular region. However this connection is not uniform, but is made differently in practically every shaman's song.[123] Qormusta Tngri alone always dwells at the centre. All this points to a world concept of the shaman in which (similarly to in the Buddhist *mandala*) each god is given a particular region to dwell in. In a shaman's song from the Küriye banner we find: 'Turning towards the four directions of the world I will pray: Tngri Lords, protect me!'.[124] This opinion is further reinforced by the fact that certain gods (*tngri*) are described as always dwelling at the door; thus Qan Kisaγa Tngri is 'at the front door',[125] and a Buryat account of Mongolian folk religion speaks of two *tngri* who guard the two doors of the world. The triple door to the West is guarded by Saγuγad Tayiji Tngri 'with only one eye in his forehead, only one tooth in his jaw and only one foot on his lower body', the middle door by the 'Lighthaired Morning Star Tngri' (Solbon Tayiji Tngri), and the outer door by Uqarima Tayiji Tngri, while the Eastern door is guarded by Köküngčüi Tayiji Tngri, 'the Lord of the Blue Hill'.[126] Baγatur Čaγan Tngri, 'Hero White Tngri' is called the 'Lord of the Western Side' and Jirüken Qara Tngri 'Heart Black Tngri' is called the 'Lord of the Eastern Side'.[127]

All of the heavenly bodies (*tngri*), whether they be deifications of the powers of nature, of abstract supernatural powers, of constellations or of natural phenomena of local significance such as high mountains or rapid rivers, have the same function: to protect the men who pray to them.

One can no longer tell what in the ninety-nine *tngri* may have descended or been borrowed from the divine conceptions of the neighbouring high religions, or which Iranian, Indian, Taoist, Buddhist, Manichaean or Nestorian Christian forms may be hidden behind the changing names of the *tngri*.

Many of them, such as the fire-god, Sülde Tngri, Dayičin Tngri, have their own cult in addition to the general calling-upon the *tngri* in incense-offerings, shamans' songs of conjuration, invocations and blessing-ceremonies, and these special cults will require separate treatment.

3 The ancestor god: the historic Činggis Khan

In Mongolian shamanism the spirits of the forefathers are worshipped because (as is clearly expressed in the Chahar shaman's chronicle[128]) they offer help against the threat to life posed by the powers of evil, forces of nature conceived of in personified form. It is, accordingly, only an adaptation of this fundamental concept of shamanism if the historical Činggis Khan too should receive such worship after his death. To this also was added, as early as the time of the Yüan emperor Khubilai, the influence of the Chinese cult of ancestors and lineage. The Chinese chronicle of Mongol rule in China, the *Yüan-*

shih, ascribes the building of a temple dedicated to worship of ancestors to Khubilai himself.[129]

In the Ordos bend, the region enclosed by the bend of the Yellow River where the Ordos Mongols have lived since the fifteenth century, Činggis Khan was and is worshipped in the shrine of the 'eight white tents'.[130] Today the shrine is accommodated in a museum-building erected for the purpose by the Chinese People's Republic.[131]

According to the Mongolian tradition, shrines for the sacrifices in memory of Činggis Khan were originally erected in the thirteenth century at four places within the Mongol Empire.[132] Today only the Ordos shrine is still known; it was very much neglected for a while in the eighteenth century, and only came back into use through the command of the Manchu emperor.[133] In 1863 Toγtaqutörü, a Khalkha prince, built a Činggis shrine in northern Mongolia, on the River Kerülün, in which the same prayers were recited in the worship of Činggis Khan as in the Ordos shrine.[134]

Independently of this, Činggis Khan was sacrificed to in all the Mongolian princely families who descended from him. This sacrifice to their ancestor corresponded to the significant procedure in many Mongolian tribes of making sacrifices to the ancestor-spirits (genii) on particular days of the year, mostly on the respective day of death. This was done in the Ordos region for the Mongolian historian Saγang Sečen (1604–62) and his even more famous great-grandfather Qutuγtai Sečen Qungtayiǰi (1540–86),[135] and on the 16 June of the lunar calendar at the grave of the ancestral lord of the Naiman Mongols in Yamen-miao,[136] among others. This shows that princely families continued to practise this kind of ancestor-worship right up to the twentieth century. However, even in the families of simple herdsmen worship and fear of the 'idol of the ancestors' remained alive, despite all persecution by the sixteenth-century Lamaist missionaries. Mergen Diyanči *bla ma* took them into consideration in around 1760 in the pantheon which he created for a Mongolian-language liturgy, again under the name of Ebügen-ü Ongγod Tngri, 'the Ancestor-Spirits Tngri'.[137] Fear of the ancestral spirits still caused the dwellers in the East Mongolian regions in our own century to use special expressions in place of the tabooed names of the ancestors; thus for example they would use *čoγ*, 'radiance, majesty', instead of *γal*, 'fire', in the name of the descendant transmitted down from the ancestor. In the East Mongolian regions last century name-tablets of the deceased, borrowed from the ancestor-cult of the Chinese, often replaced the Ongghot figures of the ancestors.[138]

Even if the precise age of the worship of Činggis Khan cannot be

10   Mongolian house-god (ancestor image), Rijksmuseum of Ethnology, Leiden

determined with certainty, the narrating of all the mighty deeds and actions of the great Mongolian ruler[139] along with the naming of his four consorts, his four sons, his brothers and his closest comrades-in-arms (*külüg*) in the context of the Činggis Khan cult indicates that here it is the historical Činggis Khan who is being invoked as an ancestor-spirit. Those who worship him and pray to him, 'Khan and Dzinong now follow old custom'.[140] The historical Činggis is, however, deified as an ancestor spirit.

> Heaven-born Činggis Khan,
> Born from the decision of sublime Heaven,
> Your body provided with heavenly rank and name,
> You who took over lordship over the world's peoples.
> Fortunately-born sovereign,
> Whose origin is from the fortunate *tngri*,
> Great in good fortune and majesty,
> You who have wisdom without instruction,
> You who rule without error . . . .[141]

He is the protective spirit of all the descendants of the lineage of the Borjigites, the Činggisids: 'You who have become the sublime genius [*sülde*] of the Borjigites, supreme among the fortunate ones, fortunate, holy sovereign'.[142] He is promoted, too, into the category of creator-god:

> Your great high tent-pavilion has become the hearth-circle
> of heaven,
> Your great broad throne is in the custody of the Earth Mother,
> My holy one, the thunderbolt of your forehead is like the
> radiance of the firmament . . . .[143]

There are only a few iconographic indications available. However, what is expressed concerning the appearance and nature of the deified ancestral lord of the Mongolian princely families coincides with the equally scanty information of the Činggis Khan gnomic poetry, going back to the thirteenth century, according to which Činggis Khan rode a horse named Ermeg Čaγaγčin, 'the Barren White Mare',[144] and wore a mantle of goatskin:[145]

> My fortunate sovereign, supreme among the fortunate ones . . .
> You who rode the white infertile mare,
> You who went wrapped in your goatskin cloak . . . .[146]

In an invocation, Činggis's eyes are described as variegated in colour, his face is white:

> My holy one, whose great multicoloured eyes are closed,
> My holy one, whose beautiful white face . . . .[147]

At the sacrificial ceremonies, especially in the Ordos region, old pictures of Činggis Khan were used, concerning which it is said 'My holy one who has become an image on jasper-white silk'.[148] On an offering-picture of this kind from Ordos, Činggis Khan can be seen surrounded by his wives and sons (Figure 11). In the 1930s the Japanese sought to replace such pictures in the areas of Inner Mongolia, which they occupied by a coloured print which showed a full-bearded, elegant, light-skinned Činggis Khan.[149]

The deified Činggis Khan was ceremonially prayed to and worshipped, along with his descendants down to the generation of the worshipping nobles,[150] without any special functions being ascribed to him, except that the ordinary people, the 'subjects, the ordinary black dogs',[151] asked him 'not to forget this prayer of the subjects'.[152] By contrast, the consort of Činggis Khan was clearly requested for long life, the blessing of children, destruction of enemies, and glory.[153] Nothing can yet be seen of any admixture of traits of a god of weather, war or heaven[154] in the figure of the deified historical Činggis Khan.

It is obvious that this deified ancestral figure would attract the interest of the Lamaist church in its attempts to incorporate the

11   Offering-image from the Ordos region, showing Čingghis Khan with his wives
and sons (after Dylykov)

Mongolian folk religion into the structure of Lamaism. The first
Peking *lCang skya* Khutukhtu, *Ngag dbang blo bzang chos ldan* (1642–1714),
composed an offering-prayer in around 1690 for the 'protective spirit
of the imperial descendants of Činggis Khan, of the Esrua of the
Earth, favoured by heaven',[155] in which he attempted to equate the
Lamaist god Sanghapala with the Činggis Khan Sülde Tngri, the

'Sülde Genius Činggis Khan'. This line of thought was taken up by one of the personal students of the first *lCang skya* Khutukhtu, *sMon lam rab 'byams pa bsTan 'dzin grags pa* of the Ujumchin, who formulated a prayer of this kind in around 1730. The Mergen Diyanči-yin Gegen also wrote an offering-prayer in connection with Činggis Khan in the middle of the eighteenth century for his national liturgy in the Mongolian language; this text was diffused widely among the Mongols[156] and was still being newly printed in Eastern Mongolia in the 1930s.[157] In this prayer Činggis Khan with his companions and ministers is requested to descend on the earth with the Yaksa and the spirits of earth and water. Činggis Khan becomes the 'White Vow-bearer' (Skt. Upasaka).

> Rest here on the place, to come to which fulfils wishes,
> On the throne made of incomparable precious things,
> On the carpet with eight glorious lotus flowers,
> Most harmonious protective spirit, white Ubasi . . .

Činggis Khan is now asked to bestow *sidi* (Skt. *siddhi*), 'magical power', on the giver of the offerings, in order to overcome all obstacles, illnesses and demons, errors and discord, and to increase good fortune and blessing, wisdom and strength! Now the great warrior and hero has found entry into the circle of protectors of the Lamaist religion, and he is asked:

> You with great power as the Khan of the Wheel of the Law
> May conquer the misbelieving wild enemy . . .
> Strengthen long life, joy, peace and strength,
> Secure for me that my actions fulfil my wishes . . . .[158]

Činggis Khan now has the same functions assigned to him as the other protective deities.[159]

> Repel curses, abuse and slander,
> On the road of war repel enemies and defeats,
> From the camp repel evildoers and enemies,
> And the enemy who opposes Master Buddha's Law
> Dismember with the strong thunderbolt-knife,
> Cut up his aorta . . . .[160]

This Činggis of Mergen Diyanči-yin Gegen's prayer has entirely become a protector of Lamaism; his special position in the ancestral cult of the Činggisids is over. How deep the influence of this Lamaized Činggis was on the figure of the Činggis Khan deity cannot be determined. In 1863 this prayer was still copied together with the old hymns from Ordos on the occasion of the new construction of a Činggis Khan shrine in the Khalkha region by

Toqtaqutörü Wang,[161] from which one can surely conclude that from the Mongolian side nothing objectionable was found in this deformation of the image of Činggis Khan.

4 The mythical Činggis Khan as initiator god

Alongside the worship of the historical Činggis Khan, founded in the ancestor cult, there are indications in the Mongolian folk-religious and folkloristic texts of the existence of a Činggis Khan figure who shows traits of a political creator-god. In other words this mythical Činggis Khan has ascribed to him the origin of various significant economic customs of the traditional Mongolian annual cycle as well as the introduction of the wedding customs of the Mongols.

The Mongolian historical tradition from the Yüan dynasty, as it is contained in the *Čaɣan Teüke*[162] ('White Chronicle'), which goes back to the time of Khubilai Khan (1260–94) and has come down to us in versions of the sixteenth century,[163] states that Khubilai confirmed once again the performance of the four seasonal festivals, which had earlier already been firm components of traditional custom. These festivals, which are closely linked with the nomadic pastoral economy, are as follows:

The Feast of the White Herd (*Čaɣan sürüg-un qurim*) on the twenty-first day of the last month of spring (April);

The Feast of Midsummer (*Jun-u aɣur-un qurim*) on the fifteenth day of the middle month of summer (June/July);

The Feast of Autumn Dryness (*Namur-un sirge-yin qurim*) on the twelfth day of the last month of autumn (eleventh month), when the foals have worn out halters and halter-straps;

Memorial Day of the Anointing of the New-Born Cinggis (*Činggis qaɣan-u miliɣad-un qurim*) on the third day of the first month of winter.[164]

The feast of the milk libation at the summer solstice[165] was already confirmed by the contemporary observations of Marco Polo.[166] The texts and addresses preserved for this occasion in the folk-religious tradition name Činggis Khan as the person who introduced this ceremony. In the formula recited at the setting-up of the wooden bowl called the 'Grey High One' (*boro öndür*)[167] for the mare's milk needed for the preparation of koumiss and for the libation the following is said:

> The blessed holy Lord Činggis Khan,
> Born at the command of Khan Hormusta Tngri,
> To conquer the twelve rulers of the foreign peoples,

Once when he struck the summer camp at the source of the
    river, at the green pastures,
He rounded up his ninety-nine white mares,
Assembled his great Mongolian people,
Drove in the great high golden halter-stake,
Stretched out the long firm halter lines,
Tied up in them the many foals . . .,
Had the 'High Brown' [milkpail] set up—,
Revering this custom I follow it,
[A custom] which has spread among his descendants,
Who have high fame, great name and title . . ..[168]

The traditions contained in the chronicle *Bolur Erike*,[169] which
was compiled in 1774/5, report in agreement with the above that
Činggis Khan

> on the cool meadows by the river, decorated with various kinds of
> flowers, had Jelme stretch the paddock-ropes and Čou-a Mergen
> of the Jürčid round up the foals. After seven days and nights had
> passed Činggis Khan himself arrived, and he declared a new law
> which had not previously been observed, in that he poured out
> mare's milk as an offering[170] to the Buddha, to the Three Jewels of
> the Teaching, and to the *tngri*, and Börte Činua Khan and the
> other ancestors who followed also offered in this way . . . .

A blessing-formula for the selecting of young cattle from the herd
and for the libation connected with it also characterizes itself as

Transmitted from the ancestors and forefathers,
Become a custom for the whole people,
Handed down from the time of the Emperor Činggis,
Become a custom for the whole Mongolian people,
The rule of the selecting of the young of cow and yak . . . .[171]

In the same way Činggis Khan is indicated in various formulae
recited in the Mongolian marriage ritual as the initiator of the
custom in question. In a marriage formula which asks after the
origin of the bridegroom we find 'This is the custom, as once when
Činggis Khan had overthrown the four foreign peoples of the five
colours and taken Börtegeljin for his wife and at that time the
dignitaries called Buyurji changed the words . . . .'[172] In the same
way another gateway-speech from Chahar is given as 'a custom
passed on from Činggis Khan'.[173]

In an East Mongolian question from a wedding-ritual, asking for
the age and name of the bride, the following pseudo-historical
passage is found:[174]

the fortunate emperor Činggis, the incarnation of Qormusta . . . at the time when he took to wife Börtegelǰin, the daughter of the Bayan of the Khunggirad, the subject of four Uγičud, sent his wise officials, led by the two ministers Buγurči and Muquli— and, following the custom of the old, the custom was fulfilled, to ask after the name and the year of birth of the bride, after the two . . . .

We find an analogous passage in a blessing-formula connected with the bow that belongs to the ceremonial wedding-clothing of the bridegroom:[175] 'the dignitary Bürinebadara created this vow [irügel] at the time when the holy Činggis Khan in his youth took Börtegelǰin Qatun to wife for eighteen years . . .'. Corresponding to this we find that a formula from Chahar which is recited at the anointing of the curtain of the bed used in the wedding-ceremony ascribes the origin of this custom too to the time and to the wedding of Činggis Khan:

Once when the holy Činggis Khan came
To the bank of the Erdeni river
To take as his consort Ghoa Setsin Khatun, perfect in virtue,
A bed-curtain of striped brocade was also drawn across,
And a skilful official spoke this formula . . . .[176]

The abundance of such ascriptions of individual parts of the Mongolian marriage-customs to a mythical Činggis Khan must have been even greater in earlier times than we can ascertain today. The East Mongolian historian Rasipungsuγ informs us in his historical work *Bolur Erike* (compiled in 1774–5), following tradition, that Činggis Khan,

when he took Börtegelǰin to wife newly introduced customs which had previously not existed. He entrusted the dignitary Dzelme from the Uriangkhai and the Tsaghadai Ebüge, who was adroit with speech, with giving gifts and a festal meal. He introduced: the anointing of the tent, the asking of the name and year of birth [of the future bride], the rendering of worship to the sun and the moon, the making up of the woman's hair and the removal of the veils [of the bride], the worship of the hearth-fire, the offering of gifts to the in-laws and honouring them, the accepting of blessing-wishes, the celebrating of the wedding-meal and other things of this kind . . . .[177]

In addition, blessings in the context of the daily life of the nomad and hunter, such as the incantation over the long straps attached to the Mongolian saddle, which are used for tying on game, refer back to Činggis Khan as the initiator of the custom: 'It is passed down by tradition that holy Činggis Khan once made an offering to the straps of his golden saddle . . . this is the reason why today the saddle and the bridle of the lord of gifts will be purified, the eight saddle-straps spoken over and a blessing recited . . . .'[178]

However, it is not only blessings, ceremonial formulae and the tradition of the chronicles that mention Činggis Khan as the initiator of custom; poetic sources make analogous statements. The ballad of Činggis Khan's two grey stallions,[179] which goes back to the thirteenth century, ascribes to Činggis Khan the custom of plaiting (Mong. *seterle*) brightly-coloured pieces of silk cloth and silk strips into the manes of the victor's horses, dedicated to the gods, at horse-races: 'The fortunate sovereign plaited pieces of silk into the mane of the little grey horse. To plait in pieces of silk, as a custom, goes back to the little grey horse, so they say . . . .'

The Mongolian tradition of legends (*domoγ*)[180] provides numerous narratives in which the reasons for the origination of customs are connected with Činggis Khan; the formation of place-names is also explained through words and items of behaviour of Činggis Khan. Thus the custom of striking the stirrups while the horse urinates is traced back to Činggis Khan, who according to the legend ordained this because once a courtier was left behind for three months on the occasion of a rapid cross-country ride because he had to stop and let his horse urinate. 'From then on the stirrups were banged when a horse urinated, and when the sound reached the emperor he made no short-cuts across fields. Because of this rule it is still today the custom of the Mongols to strike the stirrups while a horse urinates . . . .'[181]

Even if one takes into account that at the time when Central Asian tribes of riders and hunters were being restructured politically under Činggis Khan to form the Mongolian ethnic body, he must have made many rules concerning the common social life (customs partly codified by his grandson Khubilai, in particular, as is shown by the reports of the fixing of the ancestor-cult under Khubilai[182]), it is still improbable that the Mongols today remember with each of their customs its actual historical origin with Činggis Khan. This opinion is strengthened if one considers that both in a large number of Mongolian folk-religious rituals and formulae, blessings and addresses in which Činggis Khan is named as originator of a custom, and also in an equally large number in which he is not mentioned, the customs are not merely recognized as 'transmitted from ancient times';[183] their origin is, rather, traced back to the Tibetan king *Srong btsan sgam po* (620–649). Thus a handbook from Chahar[184] for the master-of-ceremonies of the wedding-feast is called 'Original Manuscript which fixed the customs for the holding of the wedding-feast at that time when, during the life of the king called the "Mountain of the Righteous, Immovable Firmament", this king gave to his son, "the righteous *Srong btsan sgam po*, possessor of ten thousand blessings, the beautiful daughter of the King of Nepal, incarnation of . . . Devi, for his wife".' In the East Mongolian questioning of the name and age of the bride, on the other hand, besides Činggis Khan there are mentioned as originators of the custom not only *Srong btsan sgam po* but also the mythical King Ardasidi from the lifetime of the Buddha Sakyamuni. A benediction on alcoholic spirits, coming from Inner Mongolia, which is also employed in the wedding-customs, mentions alongside *Srong btsan sgam po* also the mythical Indian king Mahasammata:

> Through the custom, which follows the usage of various Kings of the Law,
> Such as the wise Mahāsammata Khan of early times,
> The mighty [lord] of the Law *Srong btsan sgam po* and others . . . .[186]

The mythical Indian king Mahasammata, to whom the Buddhist tradition ascribes the origin of political thought, along with the Tibetan king and patron of Buddhism *Srong btsan sgam po*, first reached the awareness of the Mongols in the late sixteenth century, when the Lamaist missionaries, first of all the Third Dalai Lama, undertook the attempt to provide for the Mongolian princes a mythical series of ancestors that went back beyond Činggis Khan to the Tibetan and the earliest Indian kings, and thus transmitted the charisma of these rulers as promoters of Buddhism to the descendants of Činggis Khan.[187] Ardasidi in his turn, hero of a story concerning a prince, would be known to the Mongols, like King Sudadani (= Skt. Suddhodana), from the Jataka-stories of the Buddha's previous lives, which were also translated into Mongolian in the course of the Buddhist conversion.

The Činggis Khan of the traditional formulae is thus equally a mythical personality. To him was traced back the origin of customs from the grey dawn of time. Their great age, confirmed in this way, along with the reference to the creative principle (here identified with the name of a historical personality), only rendered them binding and gave them weight.

5 The deity of fire

The Mongols worship fire in the form of a fire-deity who has the functions of a god of fertility, riches and herds. The idea that fire is holy and to be worshipped is one of the oldest religious conceptions of the Mongols. Parallels for it were reported already from the

Turkic precursors of the Mongols in Central Asia from the sixth and seventh centuries AD.[188] Data attesting to the sacred position of fire also exist for the time of the Mongolian empire in the thirteenth century.

The worship of the fire-deity took place, and takes place, on one of the last days of each year[189] by means of an offering-ceremony at which the breast-bone of a sheep is offered in sacrifice, and hymns to fire are recited.[190] Today we know so many of these fire-hymns from all parts of Mongolia that by comparison, leaving aside the effects of chance, one can demonstrate the use of the same literary clichés and structural elements, and the original presence of a common prototype which must have come into existence many centuries ago.[191]

Apart from this fire-ceremony, the fire-god is also invoked several times in the course of the year in the context of smaller religious performances, which vary from place to place: in spring, to ask for blessings on the camels,[192] at the libation-offering at the time of the summer solstice,[193] at the preparation of meat for the winter provisions[194] and during a section of the marriage ceremony.[195]

The god of fire bears many names; these belong to different historical periods. The oldest term is also without doubt the most widespread: Odqan Γalaqan, which the Mongols understood as 'Youngest-born Fire-King', and Odqan Γalaqan Eke, 'Mother, Youngest-born Fire-Queen'. However, Odqan, 'youngest-born', is a loan-word from Turkish where it means 'fire-king'. The word has acquired the meaning 'youngest-born' because among the Mongols it is always the youngest son who inherits the father's yurt and along with it the paternal hearth.[196] The borrowing of the word *odqan*, 'fire-king', from the Turks indicates that the fire-cult and the worship of the fire-god were already present among the Mongols before Cinggis Khan, before the formation of the ethnic unity of the Mongols. The fire-god in its old form is feminine;[197] therefore the simplified forms Od Γalaqan Eke, Γal-un Eke = 'Fire-Mother', and Γal-un Qan Eke = 'Mother Fire-Queen' are used. There is also the term Γolumta Eke, 'Mother of the Fireplace, Hearth-Mother'. These terms are used interchangeably in the hymns for one and the same deity.

The deity of fire has the appearance of fire itself. Epithets of the god of fire are 'mother with the face of red silk, with butter as vital substance',[198] 'decorated with red silk',[199] 'my mother Od Γalaqan, who has many burning tongues, Fire-mother with a forked tongue, animated by the wind',[200] 'Odqan Γalaqan Mother, radiant like the rising sun, of the colour of dark-red bronze'.[201] She has a 'butter-face'.[202] Often she is called 'Odqan Fire-Queen-Mother, with the glow of yellow butter, with the colour of yellow feather-grass [*stipa gobica*] . . . with a camel-skull'.[203]

Odqan Γalaqan, the Fire-Mother, has 'a smoke which passes through the clouds, heat which passes through Mother Earth [Etügen]'; she 'spreads a smell of burning which rises to the ninety-nine *tngri*' and possesses 'heat that penetrates the seventy-seven levels of the Earth-Mother'.[204] Fire-Mother was 'created by Master Buddha, set alight by Qormusta Tngri'.[205] She arose 'when the Prince of Heaven [Tngri Khan] was still flat and the Princess-Earthmother [Etügen Qaγan] was still small',[206] she was 'struck on Burqan Γaldun-a', the holy mountain of the Činggisids, 'and blown into a flame on brown, wrinkled Mother Earth'.[207] There is also a mythical 'boy Aγuratai' who 'kindled her on the yellow mountain of the yellow rock'.[208]

Common to all the fire-prayers is the idea of a natural origin of the fire-deity; she had 'flint for mother, rock-iron for father, and the elm as kindling-wood' or 'grass as her red son';[209] she had 'hard stone for mother and rock-iron for father', 'Egyptian steel for father and meat-stone for mother';[210] she 'detached herself from the meadow and took her beginning from brushwood'.[211] Allusions are made only to striking fire with steel and stone, never to making fire by boring a hole.

Concerning the age of these concepts of the fire-deity, a certain dating is possible in that in one group of hymns names are given of historical personalities from the early history of the Mongols and from the family of the Činggisids: 'You who were struck by the great holy one [Činggis], you who were blown into flame by the mighty Torghon Sira . . .', 'Rich Odqan Γalaqan, struck by the holy Činggis Khan, brought into flame by the wise queen Börte Jüsin . . .'.[212] The father and mother of Činggis Khan are also mentioned in this connection: 'struck by Yesügei, the sovereign appointed by the ninety-nine sublime *tngri*, blown up by Ögelen Qatun . . .'.[213] Others named include the world-emperor Khubilai and his wife Čambui,[214] Činggis Khan's secondary wife Yesüntei of the Yeke Qorčin,[215] Čaγadai and his consort Čangqulan,[216] and also the sons of Činggis Khan, Caγadai, Ögedei and Tolui.[217] The worship of fire in general, and the fire-hymns, are described as 'the doctrine of the holy sovereign [Činggis], the example of the Empress'.[218] It is said, 'This is the learned custom, the learned scripture of the two, the Cakravartin Emperor Khubilai and the Empress Čambui.'[219]

One can deduce that this kind of special worship of fire took on its present character during the Yüan empire, and in the early Ming dynasty in the fourteenth century, after the Mongols were driven from China, in the princely families of the line of Činggis Khan. This

is also indicated by the use of the expression *dayan mongγol* (= Ta
Yüan, the Mongol dynasty, 1260–1368) in a hymn: 'when the Ta
Yüan Mongols had still not come into existence',[220] and in addition
by the use of the formulae 'I ask for good fortune and blessing for the
Chinese slaves'[221] (*boγol kitad*) and 'gold and silver, all the
property of Daibung King of the Sea'.[222] Daibung is a Mongolian
spelling for Ta P'ing, 'Great Peace';[223] only in the Yüan and Ming
dynasties did the Mongols speak of the Chinese slaves. All this
points to the thirteenth and fourteenth century as the time of the
formation of the fire-hymns, which however must have a basis which
is much older again.

Under the influence of Lamaism, and in connection with its
confrontation with the autochthonous religious forms of the Mongols,
the picture of the fire-deity changed. She became Fire Tngri (Γal
Tngri) or Fire King (Γal-un Qan). Analogously to the Buddhist
precepts (*saādhana*) through which the meditator brings about the
spiritual manifestation of the deity, the mystical syllable *ram* now
became the origin of the Fire Tngri. The Fire Tngri was now also
called Fire King Miraja (Miranča); along the paths of Tantric
magic he has taken on the form of a hermit:

> Aya, Fire-King Miranča,
> Arisen from the syllable *ram*,
> Manifested through the hermit's magic power,
> You who with pure, clear power
> Burn up that which is hard,
> You who light up the dark . . ..[224]

Buddha and the Tantric magician take over the place of the
earlier creators of fire: 'My Fire-King Miranča, created by Master
Padmasambhava, struck by the mighty Sakyamuni Buddha . . .'.[225]
Now there appears an iconographical description analogous to that
of a Lamaist deity. The red colour is still dominant, as with the Fire-
Mother Odqan Γalaqan, since 'between the Fire Tngri and the fire
itself there is no difference'.[226]

The Fire Tngri, which is also called 'Tngri of the Hearth-Circle'
and 'Mighty Tngri of the Fireplace', has the following appearance:

> From the syllable *ram* the Fire Tngri has fully appeared, red in
> colour, with one face, two hands, riding upon a brown billy-goat.
> In his right hand he holds a counting-cord and red silk strips, in
> his left hand a fire-pan. His body is decorated with various silk
> strips. Surrounded by numerous companions, the Tngri of Fire
> comes, summoned in the direction of the southern firmament . . . .[227]

Often the Fire Tngri is also called 'he who sits on the castrated billy-goat'.[228] In the Lamaized prayers to fire, the Fire King is also equated with Arsi Tngri, and he owes his origin to Esrun Tngri (= Indra), Qormusta Tngri, Bisman Tngri and Madasiri. The Fire Tngri also bears the epithet 'Yellow Fire-Tngri'.[229]

When the shamanistic and folk-religious body of ideas was suppressed, the Fire-Mother Odqan Ґalaqan was identified with the Fire King and Fire Tngri; the old body of ideas and that of Lamaism fused with one another. Mergen Diyanči-yin Gegen of the Urat Mongol tribe, noted for his attempts at an incorporation and syncretization of folk-religious traits, deities and concepts into the Mongolian Lamaist liturgy, sought in the middle of the eighteenth century to draw parallels with the fire-worship of the lands neighbouring those of the Mongols. In his fire-prayer he wrote:

> Most good and mighty Fire-King,
> Virtuous and good Arsi Tngri,
> Worshipped through offerings among the peoples of India . . .
> Fire-King perfect in majesty,
> Arsi Tngri, sovereign over all,
> Worshipped through offerings also among the people of Tibet . . .
> Fire-King whose majesty is full in every measure,
> Immaculate Arsi Tngri,
> Worshipped through offerings also among the people of China . . .[230]

Here the Fire-King and Arsi Tngri, the 'Hermit Tngri', are equated.

The attempts of the Lamaist liturgical writers to bring about a complete systematization of the old Mongolian fire-customs doubtless pursued other, hidden objects. In various old Mongolian fire-prayers, instead of a single Ґalaqan Fire-Mother there are named 'the mothers Ґala Khan, the older and younger sisters'. The Lamaist theologians, now making a borrowing from the category of Devi (Ökin Tngri) in the Lamaist pantheon, made out of this 'the seven Ökin Tngri of the hearth, older and younger sisters' and 'the female comrades of the fire, Ökin Tngri'. 'Five older and younger sisters, the Five Fire-Hearts' were also introduced.[231] The Fire-Maidens-Tngri have the appearance of wild deities from the Lamaist pantheon; a blindingly white face, two arms, a wide-open mouth with bared teeth. Four Fire-Maiden Tngri of the four cardinal points are also enumerated; the eastern one is white, the southern reddish-yellow, the western dark-red and the northern black.[232]

At the end of the eighteenth century, then, Lamaism, which had so far still retained the natural red colour of the Fire-God corresponding to the Mongols' old folk-religious conceptions, attempted to change the Fire-God's colour and thus to overcome entirely the old fire-deity.[233] In this context a prayer to fire originating and printed before 1800 in the Chahar region describes the fire-deity, Γal Tngri, in the following way:

> In the southern firmament
> Arisen from the syllable *ram,*
> In the middle of the lotus of the body of fire,
> Above the moon the Fire Tngri.
> White in colour and most gentle in appearance,
> The white knot of hair (*usnisa*) wound about the head,
> With a thick white beard,
> In the right hand the rosary of white crystal,
> In the left hand the vessel called the offering-vase, filled
>   with nectar,
> Wearing a dress of white silk,
> Sitting on a cushion made of white silk threads,
> On a lotus-throne, and around it
> Surrounded by many companions, who are like the
>   worshipped one . . . .[234]

The Fire Tngri is now given a name in distorted Tibetan, 'Fire Tngri Gugarmo'; out of the butter-faced Fire Mother is made 'the white mother with the thunderbolt'. The iconography shows the traits of a gentle deity; 'the white-clothed Fire Tngri has one face, two hands, in the right he holds a lotus-flower, in the left a carpet . . .'.[235] A Mongolian account of the customs and usages of the East Mongolian tribes speaks of an identification of the Fire Deity with the Lamaist deity Hayagriva, the protector of horses: 'in the night of the twenty-third day of the twelfth month it is the custom to sacrifice to the fire-*burqan* Hayagriva . . .'.[236]

This attempt to incorporate the fire-deity of Mongolian popular belief into the Lamaist pantheon in the form of a peaceful deity appears however (judging from the small number of manuscripts of this kind) to have gone too far and to have exercised no deep influence on the religious feelings of the Mongols. In essentials the functions of the fire-god were retained, despite all Lamaist influences, whether the god was now called Fire-Mother Odqan Γalaqan, Fire-King, Fire-King Miranča or Hermit Tngri in place of Fire Tngri. Here we are speaking of the functions of a god of fertility and protection; among a nomadic people, whose prosperity and disaster depended on the presence of warming, life-supporting fire, it could scarcely be otherwise.

N. Poppe has given a pertinent sketch of the requests directed to the fire-deity, and thus of its area of operation, in his analysis of the fire-cult:

The following requests were directed to the fire-god: the request
for blessing 'for the umbilical cord and the womb', for the birth of
a son, for long life, fame, riches and power; the request for
protection against doubt, anxiety, bad dreams and 'all sorts of
evil'; the request to drive away the *ada* and the *jedker* (as the evil
spirits were called); the request for the fulfilment of all wishes, for
protection against disagreement, discord and enmity; the request
to secure for he who prays, wherever he may be, all that is good;
the request for protection from frost and heat and from all evil
brought about by wood, fire and iron (in other words from the
elements over which he has power); the request to keep illnesses at
a distance, to preserve from slippery ice and hunger, to prevent
wolves and thieves from coming near, to protect from cattle-
plague; the request for abundant fodder for the cattle; the request
for good fortune for 'the *sür sünesün* of the horses, of the camels with
shaggy manes, of the thick-limbed bulls, of the long-tailed stallions,
of the mares with big teats, of the geldings with big swellings on
their knee-joints and of the cows with big teats'; the request for
good fortune for the *sür sünesün* of the slaves, the request on
account of *bayan kesig* 'of the loud-barking dogs'; the request to
have good friends and devoted servants and slaves; the request 'to
replace all that has died with new' . . . .[237]

The requests especially for 'sons who have grown up well, good
and beautiful daughters', for 'brides with beautiful ornament-
containers for their tresses, upright and handsome sons-in-
law',[238] are found in every invocation of the fire-deity.

From a protective deity of the family the fire-deity developed
further, in the fire-prayers of the Činggisids, the ruling Mongolian
princely families, into a god to whom was entrusted the increase and
prosperity of the people and the princes:

She who has become the mother of the five elements,
Of the subject-peoples in their thousands upon thousands . . .[239]

and

Make fortunate the ruler of the Great Empire,
King and Queen, *dzinong* and *dzaisang*,
The whole great people . . . .[240]

To the fire-deity were offered the best things which the nomadic
pastoral economy had to offer; yellow butter, melted butter and the
breast-bone of a white sheep with yellow-spotted head, the thin layer
of fat on the inside of the skin of a slaughtered beast. The breast-
bone was covered with coloured silk strips; this part of the ceremony
was therefore called 'undressing'.[241]

The use of pure butter as an offering-gift, as with the Indo-Aryans,[242] has given rise to reflection on whether connections could exist between the fire-cult of the Mongols and the fire-worship of the Indians. However, one is more inclined to derive the choice of offering from the limited possibilities of a pastoral ceremony. All indications of Indian influences in the fire-hymns of the Mongols are late introductions of Lamaism or phrases, names and legends adopted for camouflage at the time of the persecution of the old Mongolian religion and therefore originate from the late sixteenth century. The Mongols themselves speak of the fire-deity and its worship as something which is older than all other aspects of their life:

> Odqan Γalaqan Mother arose
> When Khangai Khan was still a hill,
> When the elm-tree was still a sapling,
> When the falcon was a fledgling,
> When the brown goat was a kid . . .
> When Mount Burqantu was still a hill,
> When the willow was still a sapling,
> When the lark was still a fledgling . . . .[243]

6 The 'White Old Man'

The Mongols worship under the name of Tsaghan Ebügen (White Old Man) a deity of the herds and of fertility, who is also present with the same form of manifestation and the same functions among the Tibetans (*sGam po dkar po*)[244] and the Na-khi tribes of South-West China (Muan-llü-ddu-ndzi),[245] and to whom East Asian parallels can be found in the Chinese Hwa-shang, Pu-tai Ho-shang[246] and the Japanese Jurojin, and a European parallel in the form of the bearded St Nicholas.[247] This is an instance of the veneration of the 'Old Man' as a personification of the creative principle. The Mongolians have indeed paid him literary tribute as well in their stories and humorous narratives about the 'cunning grey old man' (*boro* or *aryatu ebügen*)[248] who proves superior to all injury and all dangers.

Evidence exists of the veneration of the 'White Old Man' from practically all parts of Mongolia, from the region of the Buryats, from the West Mongolians (Oirats) and from the Volga Kalmuks.

As is already indicated by his name, the 'White Old Man' always appears in the Mongolian prayers and invocations in the form of a white-clothed, white-haired old man who leans on a dragon-headed staff: 'with a white beard and hair like one who has become old, his whole body covered with white clothes, and a firm staff in his hand with a menacing dragon at its head . . .'.[249]

In the invocations known to us the White Old Man is described as lord of the earth and of the waters, for indeed he himself makes this claim:

I lived on the mountain,
Above me the heavens as sovereign lord,
Beneath me [the Earth-Mother] Ötugen Eke as sovereign lady—
Wild animals, poisonous snakes, men and beasts,
Lords of the earth and spirits of the waters, protective spirits
    of the Empire in the twenty-four directions, however many
    and evil they may be—I can master them all;
On the mountains I am the lord of the mountain-lands,
On the steppes I am the lord of the farmlands and the waters.
Among men I am the lord of the earth, its houses and their
    waters,
In the monasteries I am the lord of the religious domain and its
    waters,
In the town I am the lord of the inhabited region and its
    waters.[250]

The figure of the White Old Man, in this its character of personified creative power, as lord of all the earth and all waters, must go back to early, pre-Buddhist times. Many things point to this.

An external symbol of this fact can be seen in the dragon-headed staff of the White Old Man, which corresponds to the horse-headed staff once held by the shaman and used by him as a mount for riding when he ascended[251] and also as a magical staff. The dragon-headed staff of the White Old Man, like the shaman's magic staff, is called *tayaɣ* in Mongolian;[252] it is only in a nineteenth-century Buryat chronicle that the *tayaɣ* of the White Old Man is made into a 'supporting stick, walking stick' (Mongolian *tulɣuɣur* or *tulɣuur*).[253] That the staff of the White Old Man is nevertheless to be understood as a shaman's staff is made clear by the beliefs of the Ordos Mongols, reported by A. Mostaert from the Ordos region, that the illness or death of cattle could be brought about by a 'blow' of the White Old Man with his stick.[254] The white clothing of the White Old Man also belongs to his shamanistic character; reference may be made here to the white clothing of Mongolian shamans at the time of Činggis Khan.[255]

The strongest evidence for the pre-Buddhist, folk-religious origin of Tsaghan Ebügen can however be found in the attempts to justify his functions made by the Buddhists when they were adopting him into the Buddhist pantheon. Certainly there is no canonical Buddhist text concerned with the White Old Man. The prayers and invocations which are known are folk-religious texts with more or less evident Buddhist interference. A pseudo-Buddhist Mongolian prayer that is dressed in the external form of a canonical sutra, and has as its Mongolian title 'Sutra able to pacify and to force into submission the earth and the water' (γajar usum-i nomuγadqan daruγulun čidaγči neretü sudur), also bears a pseudo-Chinese title with the same meaning.[256] There is however nothing corresponding to this prayer in either the Tibetan Lamaist or Chinese Buddhist canons. It counts among the most widespread Tsaghan Ebügen prayers in Mongolia.[257]

This prayer narrates the legend of the meeting of Buddha with the White Old Man and how the Old Man is confirmed in his functions by the Buddha:[258]

> Thus have I heard spoken: Once the perfectly-accomplished Buddha was walking with Ananda and the mendicant monks, Bodhisattvas and great clerics on the mountain called Jimislig, and he saw there an old man who had already reached a great age. His beard and hair had become white, he was dressed in a white garment and he held in his hand a stick which had a dragon at its head.
>
> Such was the old grey man he saw, and after he had seen him, the perfectly-accomplished Buddha spoke: 'Of what are you the Lord? Why do you live alone on this mountain?'.[259]

After the White Old Man had described to him his tasks as Lord of the Earth and the Waters, as protector of the good and punisher of the wicked, there then follows his confirmation by the Buddha:

> And when he [Tsaghan Ebügen] had explained this, the perfectly-accomplished Buddha said 'Good, good! Son of noble birth, promise in my presence to protect all living creatures . . . .'[260]

A further attempt at Buddhist justification of the figure of the White Old Man and at his incorporation into the Lamaist pantheon is found in the 'Legend of Green Tara' (Noγuγan Dara Eke-yin Tuji),[261] which was widespread among the Mongols in many copies and was very popular. One of the various episodes of this legend describes how the Green Tara blessed a 'wise, white-[haired] hermit' (mergen čaγan arsi) in the following words out of gratitude for the counsel he gave to her:

> 'Ah, although you were only an ordinary baysi in this life, in a later rebirth you will live again as the Buddha called the "White Old Man", in the form of an entirely white old man, as the lord of

the twenty-four lords of the earth and the waters, bringer of the blessing of the Three Jewels of the Doctrine, with a dragon-headed staff in your hand, ruling men and animals, as lord on the Dzimislig mountain!.' Thus she blessed him . . . This is the cause for the wandering [the existence] of Tsaghan Ebügen . . . .[262]

The attempt at a syncretic acceptance of the White Old Man into the Lamaist pantheon must go back several centuries. At least the pseudo-Buddhist Tsaghan Ebügen prayer in sutra form mentioned above must have already existed in this form before 1630, for it is found in the same words among the Mongols of Southern and Northern Mongolia, among the West Mongolian tribes of North-West Mongolia, and among the West Mongolian tribes of the Kalmuks who moved to the Volga in around 1630. In around 1760 Mergen Diyanči *bla ma*, known for having opened the way for syncretistic measures through the composition of new prayer-texts, wrote a new, and now fully Lamaized, incense-offering text himself for the White Old Man,[263] although it did not succeed in replacing the older prayers.

Although all the known surviving prayers and invocations of Tsaghan Ebügen represent him as commissioned by the Buddha, as one 'who promised and once made an oath in the presence of the mighty master Buddha to protect',[264] as 'Father, who is bound by oath . . .', and they ascribe to him the punishment of offences against the Buddhist Law, through this Buddhist adaptation there nevertheless glimmers enough of his ancient original functions and animistic-shamanistic concept. Even the idea that Tsaghan Ebügen notes down the misdeeds and sins[265] of men ('You who like Erlig Khan write down the names of those who perform various misdeeds'[266]) is taken from the Buddhist concepts of hell which had long been distributed among the Mongols through illustrated books of journeys to hell which described the horrors of hell very vividly. The basic structure of the figure of the White Old Man, going back to shamanist concepts, is nevertheless documented in the mode of punishment of the evildoers: as lord over all spirits of earth and water, 'united' with the evil powers,[267] Tsaghan Ebügen lets loose like rain upon the evildoer a hundred kinds of devils and illnesses, brigands and calumny, all kinds of wounds, evil dreams. 'They will be betrayed and nothing will be of use to them and their cattle will meet disaster and misfortune—this will I give to them'.[268] At the same time Tsaghan Ebügen is lord over life and death:

> I rule the length and shortness of men's lives, I give the
> poor the blessing of riches . . . .[269]

Here the primal creative principle is clearly personified. In accordance with this the White Old Man is also asked in the invocations and incense-prayers for long life,[270] flourishing herds and protection from the primary dangers:

> Make life long,
> Let the herds prosper,
> Destroy devils and demons . . . .
> From the danger of poisonous snakes,
> From the danger of brigands and thieves,
> Keep us far and wide . . .![271]

And in a West Mongolian incense-prayer we find:

Deign to destroy the four hundred illnesses of all living beings,
I offer a pure offering to the white Buddha-Old One, who
    destroys the terrible and great demons and devils,
Who destroys the three hundred and three sorrows,
Who destroys the eighty-eight bad omens,
Who destroys calumny and bad counsel . . . .[272]

Among the Buryats the protection of human beings is ascribed to him especially from all kinds of poxes, black and red poxes, and from various feverish illnesses.[273]

According to written prayers and oral tradition, the White Old Man descends to the earth twice a month, on the second and sixteenth days of the month, to inflict punishments and to receive the offerings presented to him.[274] The offering gifts consist of coloured silk strips and various tasty foods,[275] preferably milk.[276] The offering is made by the master of the house.

The mythical residence of the White Old Man is a mountain which is high and broad, grown over with fruit and given its name on account of this;[277] more precise geographical indications are lacking. The Buryats alone speak of the country of the White Old Man as being on the 'snowy white mountains' in the south-west, which could perhaps indicate the Himalayas.[278]

In the early Mongolian prayers and incense-offerings so far known to us Tsaghan Ebügen, as already shown, is described as an old, bearded man with a dragon-headed staff, but he is always on foot. Mergen Gegen in around 1760 was the first to attach to him a deer as mount, and in this was to relate him to Tibetan and Chinese pictorial representations which are influenced by the iconography of the Tibetan *Tshe ring drug 'khor* and the Chinese Hwa-shang and Shou-hsing. The extremely high forehead of these figures[279] was also transferred to the Tsaghan Ebügen. On older Mongolian representa-

12   The White Old Man (detail from a devotional print, Schulemann Collection, Bonn)

tions of Tsaghan Ebügen from Northern Mongolia[280] both the mount and the towering cranium are absent.

The figure of the White Old Man was admitted among the personalities of the *'cham* masked dances of the Tibetan and Mongolian monasteries; these dances in general mix up many folk-religious figures with Buddhist concepts. There too he has the appearance of a white and bearded old man. To investigate and test his role in the masked dance in order to see how far traits of Tibetan mountain deities and other concepts have here been mixed up with his figure[281] would go beyond the limits of the task fixed here; besides this would be impossible without proper studies of the Tibetan and Mongolian handbooks relating to the mystery-plays and dances, as for example the handbook of the *'cham* in Mergen Süme,[282] written in 1750 by the Mergen Diyanči *bla ma*.

7 The constellation of the Seven Old Men and the star-cult

The constellation of the Great Bear, among the Mongols mostly called the constellation of the Seven Old Men (*doluyan ebügen*), is also invoked as a god of destiny. The functions of deities of increase and fertility are also attributed to these and to other stars.

The most significant star related to this constellation is the Pole-Star, known on account of its lack of motion in the starry sky; it is called the 'golden nail' (*altan yadasun*) and also plays a special role in the celebrations of the Činggis Khan-worship in the Ordos region. There a man is buried with his feet in the earth before the tent which contains the supposed remains of Činggis Khan; he symbolizes the immoveability of the Pole-Star, and like it is called *altan yadasun*.[283] In the prayer spoken at the offering-ceremony for the imperial ancestors he is in particular instructed not to move: 'Golden Nail, do not move'.[284] It is uncertain whether this human embodiment of the Pole-Star represents a symbolical human offering, such as the Buryats used actually to offer to the constellation of the Great Bear.[285]

A prayer of request and praise to the constellation of the Seven Old Men (*doluyan ebügen*) was already translated into Mongolian and Uighur in 1328, and printed in 1330 in Peking.[286] In the colophon of the Buddhist text which was later in the eighteenth century incorporated into the collection of daily prayers (*sungdui*) and in the Tibetan and Mongolian Kanjur editions printed in Peking, the prayer is said to originate from India. It was brought from there to China, and translated then in China into Mongolian and Uighur. A translation into Tibetan, the principal language of Lamaism, first took place in 1337, from the Mongolian version.

The prayer requires the worship of the constellation of the Seven Old Men to be carried out through lights on the seventh day of the intercalary month, on the fourth day of the second month, on the fifth day of the fifth month, on the twenty-third day of the sixth month, the twentieth of the seventh month, the seventeenth of the eighth month, the twentieth of the ninth month, the seventeenth of the tenth month, the fifteenth of the eleventh month and the eighth of the twelfth stellar month.[287]

The first part of the prayer however presents clear echoes of concepts which are also found in other folk-religious prayers. The stars are spoken of as *tngri* (heavenly ones), who have their 'dwelling on the summit of Mount Sumeru'.[288] To this there is a parallel in an Ölöt legend in which the Pole-Star is anchored on the top of Mount Sumeru.[289] In the 1328 version of the prayer, the constellation is only called on in general for the fulfilment of all wishes, a long life and the pacifying of devils.[290]

In view of the widespread worship of the Pole-Star, and the formation of legends about both it and the stars of the Great Bear circling around it, among other Altaic peoples, it seems questionable whether the Mongols in the fourteenth century needed the stimulus of a prayer come from India to them through China to invoke this unalterable guiding star of the starry heaven familiar to them. It is much more likely that in this case new impulses merely met an already-present star-cult and were worked into it syncretically.

Later versions of the prayer,[291] for example one from the Buryat region, preserve parts of the old prayer of 1328, but the characteristics of an original creation of the Mongolian folk religion are unmistakable in them.[292]

The Seven Old Men have their origin

> From the family of the ninety-nine great *tngri*,
> From all the seventy-seven great earth-mothers [*etügen eke*].

It is said here

> I offer a pure offering to the stars called the Seven Old Men!
> May blessing and salvation commence here on this day!
> May this family have the joy this year of seeing little human beings!
> Graciously grant that at shooting the thumb may aim rightly, I say and offer a pure offering!
> Graciously grant that the thin saddle-ropes for the tying-on of game may be full of blood,
> That the low-dragging hems of the clothes shall be full of grease, I say and offer a pure offering![293]

The Seven Old Men are further invoked for luck at hunting, for good horses, to have a just ruler and a good leader at war, and along with them Qormusta, the prince of the thirty-three *tngri*, and Qan Jayaɣači Tngri are requested to drive away evil and suffering, devils and demons.

Fragments of incense-offering prayers which were found in the ruins of Olon Süme in Inner Mongolia show that in the late sixteenth century the invoking of constellations was usual in Lamaist prayers too.[294]

In the folk-religious prayers, however, both the individual stars of the constellation of the Great Bear, provided with their Sanskrit names, and also other stars, eventually had attributed to them the powers of a god of fertility; they were now able to multiply men and beasts, and they helped to make the herds and pastoralism prosper:

Golden Sündi, who makes a single man into a hundred men . . .,
Star Buravabadara, who makes of one mare a thousand mares . . .,
Star Aslis, who makes a simple sheep into a thousand white sheep . . .,
Star Urukini, who makes a single head of cattle into a hundred red cattle . . .,

Star Aburad, who makes one single camel into ten black camels . . .,
Star Raradi, who from one vegetable makes nine fields . . .,
Star Molbar, who makes a poor man into a rich one . . . .[295]

A special role is also played in the shamanic cult by Venus
(Čolmon), who as the morning and evening star visible at two
different times of the day is represented on many shamans' drums
not only of the Khalkha region but also of other Altaic populations.[296]

8 Equestrian deities

The Mongols worshipped a series of protective deities in the form of
armed heroes on horseback. Their task is to defend men, to keep
them from misfortune and to increase their possessions. Among
these protective deities are numbered Sülde Tngri, Dayisud-un
Tngri or Dayičin Tngri, and Geser Khan.

The iconographical form in which they appear and their protective
function both indicate connections with the Tibetan *dGra lha*,[297]
which are also of pre-Buddhist origins.[298] It is difficult to distinguish
and to describe clearly what is primarily Tibetan and what primarily
Mongolian in this, and how the influences from either side run
together here; one must doubtless suppose the existence of old
Central Asian concepts of the divine common to both cultures. In
this respect, Sülde Tngri, and the shamanistic concepts of *sülde*
connected with it, appears to be the oldest of these equestrian
protective deities, and Geser Khan the youngest.

A   Sülde and Sülde Tngri

A concept of *sülde* is already attested for the time of Činggis Khan;
according to it everyone, like Činggis Khan himself, has a genius, a
protecting companion. The oldest historical document in the
Mongolian language, the *Secret History*, speaks already in the thirteenth century of Činggis Khan's '*sülde*-possessing body',[299] a term
interpreted in Chinese as 'sign of good fortune, dignity'.[300]

The term *sülde* was also used to designate the standard of Činggis
Khan, the Tuγ Sülde consisting of nine horse's tails. Special
veneration was shown to this genius (protective spirit) of the
standard, and within the context of the Činggis Khan-cult offerings
were organized on particular days for the Black Sülde Standard
(Qara Sülde), the White Sülde (Čaγan Sülde) and the Spotted
Sülde (Alaγ Sülde)[301]; prayers and hymns relating to them have
survived. Every Mongolian prince, however, must have had such a

Sülde, because in 1911 the Sülde standard of Ligdan Khan was still being shown in Sarabči [Sarachi], near to Köke Khota,[302] and as late as the first years of the Sino-Japanese war it was the object of much skirmishing.[303] Since then it has disappeared.

The Sülde genius or protective spirit, which was thought of as established in the standard, is immortal—a shamanistic concept; the protected may well die, but never his genius. After the death of the Khan the Sülde standard continued to be worshipped until the most recent times. There also took place annual offering ceremonies for the *sülde*, the protective genius, of the respective dead person, as is shown by an example from the Ordos region in connection with the ancestor-worship directed towards the Mongolian historians Sayang Sečen (1604–? around 1662) and his great-grandfather Qutuytai Sečen (1540–86).[304] The spirit (*sünesün*) became a genius or protective spirit (*sülde*).

The following invocations show that the powers dwelling within the standards were thought of in personified form as protective spirits which were able, like the Ongghot of the shamans, to be of assistance to the descendants who called upon them.

> My great White Sülde [genius] of the sovereign [Činggis],
> You who are without fear . . .
> You who become armour for my untested body,
> Though it be delivered up to ten thousand enemies,
> You who become armour for my body of flesh,
> Though it be delivered up to thousands of enemies . . .
> My Sülde, who will help me obtain
> Booty of stallions and camels,
> Honourable wives . . . .[305]

is from a prayer to the White Standard of Činggis Khan. The protective function is even clearer, despite all Lamaist interference, in another invocation of the Sülde of Činggis Khan:

> Turn away human and non-human evil.
> Turn away calumny, rudeness and scandal,
> Turn away from the warriors terrible demons and evil-doers,
> Turn away the hateful war that causes harm to the League.
> Cut up and chop up with firm swords the enemy who is
>   opposed to the doctrine of Master Buddha,
> Tear up and cut up the artery of life! . . .
> Fall on the terrible demons and devils like lightening . . .![306]

The protective genius is called on for prince and subjects:

> . . . black Sülde,
> Deign to grant this prayer for

> Sovereign and throne,
> For the people of subjects
> And all the ten-thousands . . . ,[307]

and most especially for the descendants of the Borjigite family, the Činggisids:

> If you graciously respond to [the prayer of] the imperial
>   family, the Borjigite descendants,
> Let the evil and the envious be killed and despoiled,
> Let the golden girdle remain firm . . . .
> Let my foreign enemies be crushed,
> Let all my wishes be fulfilled . . .
> Let the hated evil-doers
> Become dust and ashes,
> Let the inherited subjects become many,
> Deign to have pity on the great people,
> Deign to have pity on the descendants themselves . . . .[308]

The particular needs of the nomadic economy are reflected in the requests made to the Sülde-genius:

> Further for the whole family,
> The babies, for so many people as there are,
> No sickness or grief, misfortune or hindrance,
> For the five kinds of herd-animal outside
> No misfortune and no wild anger, drought or famine,
> No great alarms,
> No danger from wolf or dog, no danger from the evil enemy,
>   thieves and brigands,
> Let the scanty property and the herds become greater,
> Let the glorious wind-horse-flags rise high and unfold . . . .[309]

One turns in this way, however, not only to the protective genius of the three Sülde standards of Činggis Khan, but also to the Sülde of princes, to which are ascribed the same functions, and which are invoked in exactly the same way: against demons and illness, for long life, against enemies and danger, for the increase of herds, and for blessings for posterity.[310]

The following section of an invocation of the Black Sülde standard from the Ordos region clarifies the position of the Sülde genius in the total structure of the Mongolian folk-religious pantheon:

> Holy Sülde [genius] who brings good fortune
> On campaign so that we destroy towns and fortresses,
> You who have become the lord of all people and things,
> You who took your beginning
> Through the prior decision of the holy Möngke Tngri . . . .[311]

This Sülde-genius of the sovereign, the personification of the ruler's charisma, especially that of Činggis Khan, was consequently also considered as one of the *tngri* of the folk-religious pantheon, and it appears there in the form of Sülde Tngri.[312] Thus it is called upon alongside the other heavenly beings in the most various circumstances. 'Sülde Tngri rejoices' if one worships the spirits of the booty-straps on the saddle (*yančuya*); on this occasion one asks that the 'great good fortune of the Sülde Tngri of the sovereign will be evoked'.[313] Sülde Tngri is also called upon even in the prayer to the god of hunting as 'Oppressor of the proud enemy, Sülde Tngri',[314] and Sülde Tngri is mentioned on occasion too in the invocations of the fire ritual.[315]

The equating and (at least later on) identifying of Sülde-genius and Sülde Tngri is shown by the precise offering-instruction found at the end of an invocation to Qara Sülde:

The days on which this sacrifice is to be accomplished are, each month, the first and third day of the new moon, the fifteenth and twenty-first days . . . . One goes to the peak of a high mountain. In order to perform together the incense-offering [*sang*] and the libation [*serejim*] for the holy, fortunate Činggis Khan, and to worship the *tngri* of the Golden Sülde and the Black Standard, an object of prayer [already] worshipped by the holy, fortunate Činggis Khan, it is necessary to make against insult, calumny and deception a triangular, black offering-pyramid of gold and silver filings, spirits, milk, flour and butter, and to offer a libation of black tea with a many-pointed arrow.

Against war and enemies and also hated thieves and brigands mix equal parts of all the following in spirits: blood of a man who has been killed, shavings from iron used to kill a man, and offer it with flour, butter, milk and black tea; further prepare a triangular red offering-pyramid and a triangular black offering-pyramid, all this in such a manner. If one offers these kinds of offerings without omission one can surely be master over any military actions, enemies, thieves, brigands, insult from detested opponents, and adversities of whatever kind they may be. If one however does not pay attention to the ingredients and circumstances of the offering, one will not be able to become master. Perform this incense-offering together with the incense-offering for the Black Mahakala.[316]

This last instruction already reveals Lamaist influence.

It is obvious that a deity to whom is ascribed protection from foes and their gruesome destruction through cutting up and dismembering with firm hard swords can hardly have the aspect of a peaceful, unarmed being. It is no surprise then if the Sülde Tngri appears before us, in an incense-offering prayer dedicated to him, in the following military aspect:

> White-coloured *tngri*, you who radiate light, your head adorned with a firm thunder-helmet, your armour made of the finest jewels, made of gold, drawn over your body, after that the limbs clothed with marvellous moon-boots, the quiver of tiger- [skin], filled with hard, sharp arrows, slung over the right side, the bow-holder of panther [skin], filled with the dreadful bow, hung over the left side of the body, the sharp sword girt about the hips, holding in your hand a three-pointed bamboo staff, mounted on a horse with precious saddle and harness, on your fingers an iron falcon flapping its wings upwards, leading a white lioness on the right shoulder, a great tiger crouching on the left shoulder . . . .[317]

Like all the other *tngri*, the Sülde-genius or Sülde Tngri too stands in close relation with Qormusta:

> I invoke the most mighty Sülde Tngri who was once in ancient times the object of reverence of the highest of the *tngri*, the mighty Qormusta, in order that he become the Sülde Tngri of the patron who today makes this request . . . .[318]

The systematizing and syncretizing efforts of the Lamaist church took hold of the Sülde Tngri too. On the basis of its protective functions and military appearance it fitted well into the class of *dGra lha*, 'enemy gods'. One particular 'Magic Book of the Life-fulfilling [*ayursiddhi*] Amrta Kundalin, who annihilates all demons, Praise of the Sülde Tngri, given by the Ruler of the Mysteries (Vajrapani)',[319] was translated from Tibetan into Mongolian in around the middle of the eighteenth century and distributed as a blockprint. It contains a legend about the origin of the Sülde Tngri.

Because the *tngri* were defeated in a war against the asuras, they turned to Indra (in Mongolian, Qormusta) for help. He attributed their defeat to the fact that they had no Sülde Tngri, and recommended the worship of the Sülde Tngri to them.[320] These now appeared as nine armed brothers; in this context the Tibetan *dGra lha* is translated in the Mongolian version by Sülde Tngri. Their appearance is described in the following manner:

> You Sülde Tngri, older and younger brothers, nine in number,
> Radiating white and red light,
> Mounted on [horses] as fiery as full-bloods.
> Carrying on the head the thunder-helmet,
> Clothed on the body with armour of yellow leather,
> Wearing long-legged boots on the feet,

13   Sülde Tngri (Rijksmuseum for Ethnology, Leiden)

With a quiver of tiger [skin] and a bow-sheath of panther
   [skin],
About the hips the hip-guard, girt with dagger and sword,
Holding the triple staff of reed in the hand.
Above the head the falcon flying,
A lion rearing up on the right shoulder,
A tiger springing high on the left shoulder,
Surrounded on the outer and inner sides by black gods,
   black bears and yellow bears . . . .
Incarnation of inconceivable rebirths,
For all the protectors of the White World,
Protective spirits of the doctrine, all you Sülde Tngri,
Deign to descend at this day at this place . . . [321]

The Mergen Diyanči-yin Gegen, who in the eighteenth century
took a prominent part in the creation of a Mongolian syncretistic
liturgy, described the Sülde Tngri similarly in several of the prayers
which he composed.[322] The liturgy influenced by Lamaism, also,
which has been preserved in the above-mentioned ritual in both
Tibetan and Mongolian versions, still shows the Sülde Tngri
(singular or plural) with the original functions of the armed deity

who above all 'cuts up and dismembers' evil things and dangers; for its worship weapons or an armed effigy were required.[323]

The old shamanistic concept of the ever-present protective genius also remains throughout, only now extended from the protective genius of the prince and ruler, under whose protection the whole people, noble, commoner and slave, is drawn, to the protective genius of every individual:

> Thanks to the offering to the mighty Sülde Tngri
> May Sülde Tngri not separate himself from mankind!
> Sülde Tngri, do not separate yourself from mankind,
> To whom you are bound as closely as sun and moon to
>   the firmament!
> Sülde Tngri, do not separate yourself from mankind,
> To whom you are bound as closely as the shadow to the body! . . .
> Sülde Tngri, do not separate yourself from mankind,
> To whom you are bound as closely as the fish to water.
> In the house, on the steppe, on the road,
> In these three forms,
> Wherever we go and dwell,
> Mighty Sülde Tngri, be always associated with us as a com-
>   panion.[324]

B Dayisun, Dayisud or Dayičin Tngri

Another deity worshipped by the Mongols, who also appears as a mounted warrior, is Dayisud Tngri, also called Dayičin Tngri. Dayisud Tngri is the Mongolian translation of the Tibetan term *dGra lha*, 'enemy god', and in fact iconographical representations of the nine or thirteen *dGra lha* in their military aspect are called *dayisun tngri* or *dayičin tngri* by the Mongols. Here the protective deities of an old Central Asian-Turkish realm, absorbed and systematized by Lamaism, return to their original zone of diffusion.

In this regard Dayičin Tngri, along with Sülde Tngri, appears to constitute the older form of manifestation. In a ritual for the Sülde-offering, preserved at the Ordos shrine of the Činggis Khan-cult, in a copy made at the wish of Bošuγtu Jinong of the Ordos, Dayičin Tngri is not cited in connection with the Black Sülde standard and the Sülde-genius dwelling within it.[325]

The Oirat epic concerning the deeds of Ubasi Qung Tayiji, however, the historical kernel of which is formed by an invasion into Oirat territory in 1587 by Šoloi Ubasi of the Khalkha, describes how an Oirat prisoner-of-war was sacrificed to the Black Banner Standard (*qara tuγ = qara sülde*): 'Upon this, they brought the boy forward to sacrifice him to the standard'.[326] In the benediction of the Black

Standard given here, Dayičin Tngri is mentioned:

Benevolent Dayičin Tngri, he eats and drinks,
He lets us pour out the black blood of Ubasi Qung Tayiǰi . . . .[327]

Thus Dayičin Tngri was originally connected with the Sülde-genius of the standard.

Confirming the sixteenth-century tradition, Benjamin Bergmann summarizes the results of his field research among the Volga Kalmuks in 1802–3 as follows: 'Daitsching tängäri. This divine being is the war-god of the Mongols and Kalmuks. On campaigns he is carried before the army, represented on standards. Sometimes captured enemies are sacrificed to him.'[328]

However, there are no further reports concerning Dayičin Tngri and either his relationship to the standards or his connection with the human sacrifices offered to the standards. There are certainly other indications besides those in the epic of Ubasi Qung Tayiǰi that the Mongols sacrificed prisoners-of-war to the Sülde standards. The *Man-chou shih-lu*, the 'True Annals of the Manchu Dynasty', relates under 1620 a report that Ligdan Khan of the Chahar (1604–34) had 'killed and offered to his standard' a messenger of the Manchus.[329] Even at the time of the war of independence of Northern Mongolia from the Chinese in 1911, prisoners-of-war were still being sacrificed to the standard.[330] In this connection, the contemporary Mongolian poet and scholar B. Rinchen cites in his historical novel *Rays of the Dawn*[331] not from a prayer to Dayičin Tngri, but from a prayer to the Black Sülde[332] and the Sülde-genius.

In this respect the citation given above from the instructions for the offering to the Black Sülde [-genius] is significant, in that it prescribes as one of the ingredients of the offering 'the blood of a man who has been killed'.[333]

References to the sacrifice of captured enemies are also found in an invocation of Geser Khan. Even if we are concerned here with demons and enemies of the Buddhist religion, it can nevertheless be concluded that the knowledge of this custom, and of its use in connection with military campaigns and the sacrificial ceremonies connected with them, is present in latent form:

Aya, in former times,
When the black devil who oppressed the Buddha's law was destroyed . . .,
His heart was torn out and sacrificed to the *tngri* . . . .[334]

The names and conceptions of the various war-gods and protective gods, Dayičin Tngri, Sülde Tngri and the Tibetan *dGra lha* became more and more confused with each other. A strong contribution was

14   Dayičin Tngri (Portheim Foundation, Heidelberg)

made to this by translations into Mongolian of Tibetan prayers which called upon and described the *dGra lha* in their military aspect. Especially to be mentioned here are the invocations to Dayisun Tngri composed in the seventeenth century by the Fifth Dalai Lama (1618–82)[335] and by the first Peking *lCang skya* Khutukhtu, *Ngag dbang blo bzang chos ldan* (1642–1714).[336] These received rapid and widespread diffusion among the Mongols. The latter lama gave a description of the 'Great Sovereign of the Enemy Gods' exactly like that of the Sülde Tngri in other prayers:

> In the firmament sat in front, like to a mountain of snow, the high prince of the enemy-gods, who has magic power, as if riding on white clouds, on a high, choice and noble horse, holding the lance which takes the enemies' lives in his right hand, in his left hand the blade which reaches the evildoers, and ornamented with fluttering ribbons and jewels . . . .[337]

Dayičin Tngri's dwelling in the clouds is an old shamanistic concept; in the invocation of the local mountain-deity Dayan Degereki we already find 'Dayičin Noyan Tngri, who ascends the seventy clouds'.[338]

Further evidence for the confusion between the gods named Dayičin Tngri, Dayisun Tngri and Sülde Tngri is provided by the fact that in an invocation of Dayisud Tngri, the 'Enemy-Gods', the whole wording of an invocation of Sülde Tngri[339] is simply taken over:

> Always bound as a companion like to the shadow . . .
> Wherever we go, wherever we dwell.[340]

The syncretistic influence of Lamaism is seldom expressed as strongly as in the complex of deities in equestrian form, where an amalgamation took place of old ideas with figures from the Lamaist pantheon which had themselves earlier penetrated the Lamaist pantheon from a pre-Lamaist layer of ideas.

C   Geser Khan

The third equestrian deity worshipped by the Mongols is Geser Khan. He is a protective deity of warriors and of herds, especially the herds of horses, and he also bestows good luck at hunting. In one of the many Mongolian incense-offering prayers addressed to him we find

> To Geser, Khan of the ten regions of the world, I offer a
>   pure sacrifice,
> To him who on campaign destroys the evil enemy,
> Who at hunting grants that one finds game,
> Who fulfils all my wishes in my work connected with
>   the herds . . . .[341]

Power over demons and devils is also ascribed to him. He is both 'the destroyer and oppressor of the angry demons' and also the force which 'grinds into dust the enemies and devils who alarm the state and religion'.[342] He is implored:

> Grant that at the time of the festival the wind-horse [flag] may
>   unfurl,
> That at the time of shooting the aim may be good,
> That at the time of battle strength may be increased . . .[343]

and also

> Make the State and religion, the two, strong!
> Make me the first in the festal games!
> Let us enjoy happiness and peace!
> Deign to give the gifts of long life and profit at trade!
> Grant that when rounding up or driving game that we meet wild
>   game-animals and that the saddle-ropes are full of spoils . . . .

Cause curses, calumnies and oaths to be extinguished,
Let things we desire happen as we imagine!
Deign to hunt far away foes and robbers, along with evil,
   spiteful beasts of prey and wolves . . . ![344]

Geser Khan is invoked as a protector:

Deign to annihilate the devils and demons,
Deign to make life last long,
Deign to give the grace of possession . . .
Through the power of this pure offering made with prayers![345]

One makes offerings to him because he is 'the supporting-beam of the dwelling-house and the railings of the cart'.[346] His protective function emerges especially clearly in invocations like the following:

Ah, my holy Geser-Sovereign, you who
In danger from fire are like water,
In danger from storm are like a mountain,
In danger from water are like a boat,
In danger from enemy like a lightning-flash, to you,
To the holy Geser Khan who is so mighty, I make a purifying
   offering![347]

Or:

To you I offer a pure offering,
You who are support and help for my fearful life,
To you I offer a pure offering,
You who are armour for my hairy body . . . .[348]

Finally, Geser Khan is also requested for protection and good fortune for the ruler and the princes themselves: 'May you graciously protect the vow of the ruler!'[349] We also hear, in connection with the wind-horse flag (kei mori), the symbol of good fortune for tent and settlement:[350] 'Graciously allow the wind-horse flags of the ruler to arise and unfold like a cloud in summertime.'[351] Most of the requests however are concrete: 'Deign to protect the flocks and to guard them from being lost to the enemy',[352] and

Through the merit that results from the offering to the tngri,
Let no feverish illness come to the human beings,
Let no harm come to the flocks,
Let the danger of hail not come to the fruits of the fields,
May we not befriend evil-minded companions,
May we not be overcome by hostile armies and brigands . . . .[353]

Geser Khan however has his home 'above the high white rocky

peaks in a house of cloud and mist'. He is regarded as 'Son of Heaven'[354] or as 'incarnation of the *tngri* who rule all those who live on the earth',[355] though he is also called 'embodiment of Garuda',[356] or the king of the birds.

This function of protective deity of flocks and property, of health and long life, is unimportant however compared to Geser Khan's function as a war-god. In this role he has entrusted to him primarily the protection of the warrior, the attainment of victory over his enemies and their destruction. In this connection he is omnipresent:

> In whatever direction I may go
> You go angrily above in the blue sky,
> Below you surround Mother Earth,
> You who kill all enemies and defeat them totally,
> When blazing fire sprays from your mouth,
> When you throw the golden spear from your hand,
> You who hack down and oppress the enemy . . . .[357]

Geser Khan is the actual leader of the warriors in a symbolic sense:

> In the campaign for booty,
> Deign to be the leader of those greedy for booty,
> When the whole people sets forth in train,
> Deign to be the lord of all the people . . . .[358]

In this role offerings are made to him and he is requested for victory and booty:

A pure offering for Geser,
Who has become the leader of the army,
A pure offering to him,
Who in the land of the foe has become prince of the warriors,
Deign in the foe's land
To lead the warriors in attack . . .
Allow us to penetrate into the camp of the mighty foe,
Allow us to destroy and annihilate country and town of the
    enemy in a swift campaign,
Allow us to destroy, annihilate towns and villages of the enemy.
Allow us to kill the mighty enemy,
Allow us to inflict an end on the hated enemy,
Allow us to gain much booty from the people, property and
    horses of the enemy,
Allow my companions, and I who invoke you, to gain much
    booty from the belongings and flocks of the foe . . . .[359]

Similarly we find in a West Mongolian invocation:

Let me gain power over the sons of the evil foe and kill them,
Guard and protect my flocks . . . .[360]

The Geser Khan invoked in these prayers has the uniform
iconographical appearance of a warrior on horseback, of Central
Asian-Iranian origin, such as we already meet in the wall-paintings
from Turfan:

> with a reddish-brown face, a golden-yellow top-knot of hair
> [*usnisa*], with one head, two hands, in the right hand holding the
> arrows with the sign of Garuda, in the left hand the bow with the
> tiger's sign, on his head the sun-like helmet is placed, the moon-
> like shield hangs over his shoulder, the star-like coat of mail is
> drawn over his body, the fine sword of understanding is raised in
> his hand . . . riding on the horse of wisdom.[361]

Or similarly:

> The golden armour drawn over his body,
> His forehead decorated with the helmet of crystal on all eight
>   sides,
> The quiver of tiger-skin on the right side of his body,
> The arrows like lightning and shooting-stars,
> The bow-holder of panther-skin slung over the left side of his
>   body,
> Holding the splendid white-edged bow,
> The sharp sword with the handle ornamented with jade and gold,
> Holding a spotted antelope in the right hand,
> Holding the golden rein in the left hand,
> Riding on a horse whose saddle and harness are of jade . . . .[362]

Despite occasional liberties of poetic expression, the picture of the
god remains basically the same:

> Geser, lord of the four kinds of warriors,
> White-coloured light shines from his body,
> His head is covered with a great jewel-helmet,
> The King of Birds, Garuda, fixed on the helmet,
> His head visibly ornamented with sun and moon,
> The coloured iron armour drawn onto his body, . . .
> Girt with the belt ornamented with great jewels,
> Swinging the lance with the red flag in his right hand,
> Grasping the golden rein in his left hand,
> The horse armoured . . .
> The tiger-quiver hanging on the right side of his body,
> The bow-holder of panther-skin on the left side . . . .[363]

This uniform picture of Geser Khan in the Mongolian invocations and prayers closely approaches the forms in which are represented the Lamaist gods Kubera (= Vaisravana, Bisman Tngri) and *dPe har* on the one hand, and the four Lokapalas and the group of the *dGra lha*, the 'enemy-gods',[364] on the other side. All of these deities show the traits of armed horsemen and ancient Central Asian influences can be determined for all of them.[365] In fact, the Mongolian Geser Khan-deity is also identified with *lCam sring* = Kubera, if in a somewhat restrictive manner: 'We praise and make offerings to you who are called incarnation of Jamasaran [*lCam sring*]'.[366] Relationships open up too towards the Sülde Tngri/*dGra lha*: 'Holy Geser, you who became a protector [*sülde*] of my exhausted body',[367] or 'Protect me like a shadow while I stay in the house'.[368] These however seem to be more recent equivalences, made from the Lamaist side, which explained Geser in terms of the *dGra lha* in the context of Tibetan folk religion too,[369] thus admitting him into the extensive group of protective deities.

The Geser Khan of the Mongolian folk religion shows many parallels with the Geser Khan of Tibetan folk religion. In both cases he has similar iconographical characteristics.[370] Tibetan folk religion also recognizes a deification of the companions and opponents of Geser Khan who are mentioned in the Geser Khan epic.[371] This points to connections between the Geser Khan cult and the Geser Khan epic. While the deification of the companion and opponents of Geser Khan is lacking in the Mongolian Geser Khan cult, on the other hand the figure of Geser Khan in Mongolian folk religion unites the functions of a protective deity of property and of the herds with those of a warrior-god. In addition close relationships appear with the Geser Khan epic in its Mongolian versions.

In the first place, the iconographic description of the person of Geser Khan uses the same emblems and epithets as occur in the Mongolian Geser Khan epic. In both, Geser Khan wields the sharp sword of understanding. In the epic his white helmet is adorned with sun and moon; in many prayers of the Geser Khan cult, Geser Khan wears the sun as a helmet-ornament, while another group of prayers describes Geser's helmet as made of rock-crystal and ornamented with the Garuda. The moon decorates Geser Khan's shield. It is noteworthy that the Tibetan bards of the Geser Khan epic still today in the Tibetan border-region wear pointed hats decorated with the sun and the moon.[372] In addition to this however there are, in the numerous Mongolian prayers to Geser Khan, always references to events that are recounted in the Mongolian (and in many cases also in the Tibetan) Geser Khan epic. Geser in the prayers as in the epic is given the epithet 'Geser Khan, so redoubtable that he cuts and

destroys the roots of the ten evils of the ten parts of the world'.[373]
Reference is made to the description, which occupies a prominent
place in the epic, of Geser Khan's combat with the Sirayiγol Khans
and their killing by him. Geser is called he 'who killed the Siraighol
Kings'.[374] The killing of the twelve-headed giant by Geser, also the
principal episode of one of the songs of the Geser Khan epic, also
finds mention: 'He who conquered the twelve-headed giant enemy,
who resides as sovereign among the Mongol people, to the tirelessly
valiant Geser Khan with a body like rock-crystal I make a pure
offering!'.[375] Finally, Roγ mo, the beautiful wife of Geser Khan,
who is often named in the epic, is mentioned in the prayers: 'I make
a purifying offering to the beautiful consort Roγ mo';[376] to Geser it
is said, 'you who have a beautiful wife'.[377]

The companions of Geser Khan from the epic are also drawn into
the circle of those who are invoked:

> A purifying offering to the valiant heroes, the mighty
> companions,
> A purifying offering to the most fortunate companions and
> servants.[378]

The number of the thirty five heroes and three-hundred and sixty
warriors of the vanguard (qusiγuči) of Geser Khan cited in the
invocations[379] is also taken from the Geser Khan epic, where the
number of heroes varies between thirty and thirty-five. Many even
of the poetic epithets of the epic, such as 'you who are light to me in
the dark night'[380] reappear in the Geser Khan prayers: 'I offer my
pure offering to you who in dark night are to me a bright light'.[381]

All this indicates that the worship of Geser Khan as a protective
god and war-god, and the origin of his cult among the Mongolians,
is closely connected with the becoming-known of the motives and
legends of the Tibetan Geser Khan epic among the Mongols. Since
this must have happened at around the end of the sixteenth and
beginning of the seventeenth century, as emerges from a prose
version translated from Tibetan in around 1614[382] we can derive
from this a dating for the beginning of the Mongolian worship of
Geser Khan. In none of those folk-religious prayers which go back to
very ancient prototypes and traditions, such as the fire-prayers or
anointing-blessings,[383] is Geser Khan mentioned among the names
of the ancient shamanist tngri. He is evidently a relative newcomer in
the folk-religious pantheon of the Mongols. As a consequence of the
familiarity of his form of manifestation, as a warrior-god and as a
warrior on horseback, he must have gained in popularity quickly,
and indeed to the same degree as the suggestions and themes of the
Tibetan Geser Khan epic developed into the individual Mongolian

version of the Geser Khan epic. The hero of the epic, 'the helpful, holy Geser Khan, born in order to cut and destroy the roots of the ten evils of the ten parts of the world', sent by the ruler of the heavenly beings (*tngri*) to fight against injustice in order to help mankind, offered himself by virtue of this commission for the role of a protective deity. A Mongolian description of the development of shamanism among the Eastern Mongols,[384] which because of its mention of events from the time of Ligdan Khan and the first two Manchu emperors must have originated in the first half of the seventeenth century,[385] gives a picture of the religious forms of this period among the Mongols. Here it is said that 'some, carving a man and a horse out of wood, placing the man on the horse and putting a sword in the hand of the carved wooden man, make a figure and make offerings to it . . . .'[386] By 1716 the Geser Khan epic was already so well known among the Mongols that Emperor K'ang-hsi, as part of the Manchu policy of friendship towards the Mongols,[387] had a Mongolian blockprint edition made in Peking of the first seven chapters.[388]

During the eighteenth century one characteristic of the Manchu policy on religion emerged ever more clearly: 'to bring about a fusion between Lamaist and Chinese religious concepts and ideals'.[389] Here too lies the cause for the latter identification of Geser Khan with the Sino-Manchurian war-god Kuan-ti. The worship of Kuan-ti, the Chinese hero of the third century AD who had been raised to the status of the Chinese god of war, had already begun to spread under the emperors of the preceding Ming dynasty in China, especially under the Ming ruler, Shen-tsung (Wan-li) (1573–1620),[390] and the Manchu also adopted Kuan-ti as a god of war. The Manchurian translation of the Chinese historical novel *San-kuo-chih* ('History of the Three Kingdoms'),[391] which was already made in 1647 and distributed in printed form, doubtless played a decisive part in this process. This novel narrates the heroic deeds of Kuan-yü (= Kuan-ti); in the seventy-seventh chapter his deification is described.[392] In the middle of the eighteenth century, at the request of the *rJe drung* Khutukhtu, an offering-prayer for Kuan Lao Yeh[393] was composed by the highest Lamaist dignitary at the Imperial court of Peking, the *lCang skya* Khutukhtu *Rol pa'i rdo rje* (1717–86). This prayer was distributed widely in Tibetan, Manchu and Mongolian versions. In it Kuan-ti, the old Chinese god of war, is declared to be the 'great protective deity [*yeke sülde tngri*, corresponding to the Tibetan *dgra lha*] of the Chinese Empire', and is brought into connection with the leading triad of deities of the *dGe lugs pa* sect, Guhyasamaja, Cakrasamvara and Yamantaka. Kuan-ti is here invoked for the 'spreading of the Buddhist religion and the pacification of those who live in the [Chinese] Empire'.

In this eighteenth-century prayer to Kuan-ti, Geser Khan is still not mentioned. The name of Geser is not found either in other Tibetan prayers of the same time which are dedicated to Kuan-ti (such as the description of his ritual, *Kwan po yi bzog ma*,[394] or the *Chos spyod bsrungs ma bkwan po yi'i gtan rag chod pa*[395]), let alone the equating of Geser with Kuan-ti.

In the late eighteenth century and up until the late nineteenth century, especially under the Manchu Emperors Chia-ch'ing (1796–1820) and Tao-kuang (1821–50),[396] the Manchus covered the border provinces of the Chinese Empire, and their original homeland, Manchuria, with Kuan-ti temples, in which he was worshipped in his role of protective deity of the state and military god of the Manchurian soldiers and functionaries.[397] In Kansu, Mongolia, Sinkiang and Tibet alone sixty-five temples for Kuan-ti were built through state subsidies with this end in view.[398] At the same time Kuan-ti, the former Chinese war-god, was allowed entry into the Lamaist pantheon by the Lamaist church. Kuan-ti was equated with *lCam sring* (Skt. Kubera/Vaisravana), with whom Geser Khan had already been identified from the Lamaist side. The iconographic similarity of the two, as warriors, led to a further step taking place, and thus it came about that in the Kuan-ti temples of the border region on the trilingual name-inscriptions there took place the equating of the 'holy great sovereign Kuan' with the 'holy Geser Khan of the Kuan family',[399] a step entirely consonant with the policy of fusion pursued during the Chia-ch'ing and Tao-kuang eras.

Taoist divinatory practices, which had already become connected at an earlier stage with the Chinese war-god Kuan-ti, were now transferred to Geser Khan too. A Mongolian witness in a handbook of divinatory signs from the twelfth regnal year of the Emperor Chia-ch'ing (= 1807), speaks of the widespread custom 'of imploring for a heavenly omen in the temples of the Great Holy Khan, Dayisun Tngri [= Kuan-ti], now built everywhere, and in the temple of the Holy One built in the Yung-ho-kung . . .'.[400] Divinatory texts with predictions of Kuan-ti for the coming year were widespread too in the Mongolian language, and, in the form of chain-letters, promised those who copied them liberation from coming dangers.[401]

A little later the Kuan-ti oracle was equated not only with the Dayisun Tngri (Tibetan *dgra lha*), but also with Geser Khan.[402] These divinatory practices in the name of Geser were subsequently used even in Tibet.[403]

Up until the second half of the nineteenth century Lamaist Mongolian theologians such as the Ilaγuγsan Khutukhtu Mergen Bandida *Don grub rdo rje* (1820–82) worked for the further fusion of the figures of Kuan-ti, Geser and the Dayisun Tngri[404] and made out of Geser Khan a protective deity of the Buddhist religion. This however represents a late stage of development.

For the Mongolian people on the other hand Geser Khan remained the equestrian warrior-god, with traits taken from the folk epic. The syncretic arrangements remained without deeper effect. Occasionally, it is true, the title of a copy of an older Geser Khan prayer would now give the name of Kuan-ti in place of that of Geser Khan, without otherwise altering the previous wording;[405] the Mongols regarded the Kuan-ti statues in the temples of the Manchu state god and god of war as representations of their beloved hero Geser Khan.[406] In the invocations of East Mongolian shamans, Geser Looye Burqan was included among the *tngri* to be invoked for assistance.[407] In his role of protective deity of the Mongols, guarding against harm to the flocks, from weather and from illness, the Geser Khan of the Mongolian Geser Khan epic continued to be worshipped up until the 1930s, at least among the East Mongolian tribes, in particular in the fully sedentary Küriye banner. Until 1945 there were special Geser Khan chapels there in the farmsteads of the more prosperous Mongols, with wooden statues of the hero on horseback. The Geser Khan epic was widely distributed in many impressions from the 1716 blockprint edition and in beautiful manuscripts agreeing with the printed version. On occasions of illness, threatening danger and sickness in the herds, parts of the epic were recited by Lamaist monks. The texts of the epic were treated with great respect, and had always to be kept in a horizontal position in a 'pure' place, in order not to anger Geser Khan. When the author borrowed some of the manuscripts from the Küriye banner in 1943 in order to compare them with the printed version of 1716, the owner requested them back after only a few weeks, since animals were sick and it was wished to use the texts to cure them; at the same time the illness was ascribed in a general manner to having allowed the texts to be removed.[408]

9 The cult of the earth and the cult of heights

According to the Mongols' animistic mode of thought, the entire earth was animated by good and evil powers, personifications of deceased ancestors.

The travellers of the Middle Ages already report that the Mongols worshipped a personification of the earth as a deity. Marco Polo has the following to say on this subject:

they have one of their deities, whom they call Natigai, and they say that this is a deity of the earth or god of the country, who protects their women and their sons, their flocks and their grains . . . and they show it great worship and reverence, for each keeps an honourable place for it in his house. They make this god, namely, out of felt and from other materials . . . .[409]

This deity called Natigai is the Etügen Eke of the Mongols,[410] called Itoga by Plano Carpini.[411] Between her, the ruler of the Golden World (*altan delekei*), and Heaven, there exists a fertile polarity, from which all things proceed:

Above the ninety-nine *tngri* . . .
Below the [Earth-] Mother Etügen of seventy-seven
    levels . . . .[412]

Etügen Eke (Earth-Mother) is called 'brown-wrinkled Mother Earth' (*boro körösütü etügen eke*), often also 'brown-wrinkled golden world'.[413] Homage is rendered through libations[414] to this earth which protects all and bestows on all. Further indications concerning the early ritual of earth-worship are lacking.

Earth and water, the mountains, heights, lakes and rivers of the Mongols were thought of as animated by powers, the Lords of the Earth (*γajar-un ejen*) and the Lords of the Water (*usun-u ejen*). Already at an early stage Lamaism took over these local deities; the incorporation of the local deities of the Tibetan *Bon* religion into the system of the Lamaist cult offered a useful precedent for such a procedure. The oldest surviving incense-offering prayers to the Lords of the Earth and Water, from the sixteenth century, already show traces of Lamaist influence.[415]

Above all it was the heights and mountains that counted as dwelling-places of Lords of the Earth and mountain-spirits. These were responsible for the well-being of the people living in the respective regions and the well-being of their flocks. The awe of the Mongols for these mountain-deities was so great that in ordinary speech one never used the actual name of the mountain, but referred to it by laudatory circumlocutions such as 'the beautiful' (*qayirqan*), 'the holy' (*boyda*), 'the high' (*öndür*) and so on.[416] The actual name of the mountain was taboo.

The mountain Burkhan Galdun was already in the time of Činggis Khan regarded as being especially holy and rich in protective power. According to the *Secret History of the Mongols*, the oldest epic chronicle of the Mongols, transmitted from the thirteenth century, Činggis Khan prayed to the mountain of Burkhan Galdun, which had bestowed protection on him and on his forefathers, in the following manner:[417]

Through Burkhan Galdun my life,
Otherwise worth no more than filth, is protected.
I have experienced great anguish!
Each morning I will worship
Burkhan Galdun through offerings,
Every day I will pray to him!
Let my children and children's children keep it in mind!

The ritual belonging to this is performed by kneeling down nine times and strewing about offerings to the sun with one's belt hanging about one's neck, and one's hat on one's hand.[418]

This example from the early history of the Mongols shows how a mountain has come to take on a special place as an object of worship. The custom of burying ancestors and important persons side by side on high places further contributed to the development of concepts of a mountain having life in an animistic sense. The Chahar shamanist chronicle narrates how the corpse of a dead ancestor was interred on a high place and how there resulted an association of ancestor-spirits and natural powers:

he buried the corpse on the summit of a flat rock on the southern slope of the Red Rock (*ulayan qada*) which rises up high on its own . . . . After about three years had passed during which he performed worship, clouds and mist gathered over the peak of the Red Rock, rose high and dispersed . . . . Thereupon the spirit of the deceased old father united itself in friendship with the Lords of the Place and the Lords of the Earth . . . .[419]

The *Secret History* too tells of the burial of the dead halfway up the slopes of mountains which were famous and visible from afar.[420] This custom of burial on heights can already be attested for the Stone Age in Mongolia, as is shown by the example of the Ulayan Qada (Red Rock; Chinese Hung-shan) near to the East Mongolian town of Lin-hsi in Chi-feng Hsien; on this mountain various levels of Stone Age burials were found.[421]

Stone cairns (*oboya<obo*) in particular places, mostly heights, passes or cross-roads, enjoyed special veneration as dwelling-places of the local protective deities and the Lords of the Earth. The custom of marking out particular high places through such stone cairns is found among many Central Asian and Altaic populations.[422] In a Mongolian account of the custom we find:

In early times, when there was still no Buddhist religion in the land of the Mongols, one made places, in order to invite the Lords of the Earth and protective spirits to all holy sites, mountains and lakes, to these places, and for the offering-ceremony one made

103

15   Stone *obo*

ornaments for the places, by erecting *obo* and arranging them in a decorative manner . . . .[423]

The *obo* also served, in the context of the shamanist conception, as the dwelling-place and gathering-point of the local spirits.

No prayers have survived for the *obo*-cult and the related worship[424] of the local-gods and mountain-gods which are free of Lamaist interference. This circumstance shows on the one hand with what intensity Lamaism took on the transformation and fusion of precisely these most ancient and characteristic ideas of Mongolian folk religion, and on the other hand it points to the great age of these animist concepts. Already in the middle of the eighteenth century the famous creator of a Mongolian national liturgy, Mergen Diyanči Lama, had difficulties in obtaining old texts on the *obo*-cult. In his introduction to the worship of *obo*, which is found in his collected works,[425] he says

> Now there has been a great deal of chatter in our land about the erection and worship of *obos*, and so on, and it is rumoured that there was an ancient rite, but so much apart, this ancient rite was never widely diffused in our country, and no original text of it has been seen, nor have books of regulations been composed by learned scholars in our own quarter. Though there was an ancient Mongol text from olden days, it would be difficult for its practical application and reading to be understood . . . .[426]

What can be reconstructed from the surviving old texts concerning the form of the *obo*-cult is then to a greater or lesser degree a Lamaist adaptation of old shamanistic concepts, which here have been cut about and altered more than is the case with other folk-religious expressions of more recent times. The Lamaist liturgical writers subsequently made the shamanistic local deities and the Lords of the Water into gods and dragons and the eight classes of Lords of the Earth and Water, in an analogous way to the systematization of Tibetan folk religion and its nomenclature of *sa bdag* (Lords of the Earth) and *klu* (dragons).[427] Mergen Diyanči formulated this as follows:

> ... *obos* in this land of ours are made as a shrine and receptacle in which will dwell the gods [*tngri*] and dragons [*luus*] and eight classes of the lords of land and water, who are a protection, enclosure, aid and tutelary genius [*sülde*] for ourselves ....[428]

However, despite all the Lamaist additions, and the incorporation of the deities which were invoked into the Lamaist pantheon, the protective function of the local deities remained the same in the *obo*-cult as in other expressions of folk religion. In the 'Praise of the *Obo*' (*oboyan-u maytayal*), spoken at the conclusion of the *obo*-ceremonies, and taken according to Mergen Diyanči Lama from 'an old Mongol text',[429] we find:

> We adore the gods [*tngri*] and dragons, the protectors and tutelary geniuses who accomplish perfectly our desires when we offer prayers and offerings .... Through the strength of this our obeisance, worship and praise do you constantly be companions and friends to us all, sacrificers and those on whose behalf sacrifice is made, at home or in the steppe or wherever we may be. Allay illness and the hindrances of *ada*- and *jedker*-demons; spread the splendour of long life and the joy of felicity; ... banish all the tormenting, inimical *todqar*-demons; banish all plague and epidemic illnesses, and ills of day, month and year; avert evils of the type of wolves attacking the flocks, thieves and brigands stirring abroad, hail, drought or cattle-pest occurring ....[430]

Alongside the local spirits and deities manifested in the *obo*, the spirits and personifications of individual mountains and rivers are also worshipped. Above all the prominent mountains of Northern Mongolia such as the Altai,[431] Khangai, Kentei, Bogdo Ola, Bayan Jirüke, Songgina, and Mount Čenggeltü in the Altai, and the South Mongolian Alashan and the Muna Khan are worshipped in invocations of their own.[432] The rivers Selenga, Onon, Kerulen, Ili and Irtysh, and the South Mongolian Khatun Ghol (Huang-ho) have the same honour.

> To Altai Khan and the holy Qoboq Sayiri, to
> Mount Alay, to the Irtysh, Emil, Boro Tala and
> Ili, to the Khans who protect and
> Shelter me, to all the
> Lords of Earth and Water,
> To all the Lords of this particular place,
> We give the first-fruits as offering,
> We invite you respectfully to come here . . . .[433]

is taken from an invocation to the gods of Dzungaria. In a prayer to
the mountain gods of the Altai the following is said:

> I offer a pure offering to all the thirteen Altai [mountains],
> I offer a pure offering to the thirty Kükö [mountains],
> May a pure offering be accomplished . . . ![434]

The protective functions here attributed to the mountain-spirits
are similar to those for which the Lords of the Earth are requested in
the *obo* cult:

> Grant that year after year will turn out well for me,
> Let my life be long,
> Grant that my cattle and my herds become many! . . .
> Destroy for me all illness, demons and devils,
> Let there exist for me fair concord and peace,
> Grant that riches and blessings unfold for me . . . ![435]

And elsewhere:

> Let me have good friends,
> Keep brigands and thieves away
> On the steppes and on the roads.
> Let the three worlds be under my power . . . ![436]

An incense-offering for the mountain-spirits of the Kentei massif,
although coloured by Lamaism, contains similar requests:

> Govern the weather of the seasons,
> Let seeds, fruits and saps increase,
> Let all favourable actions proceed unhindered!
> Deliver us quickly from the fear of inundation,
> Of the flooding-over of rivers and waters,
> Making showers of rain, thunder and hail and
> Hindrances to the use of beasts of burden and riding-beasts
> of the lama and his novices cease . . . .[437]

The spirits of the North Mongolian mountains Čenggeltu, Bayan
Jirüke, Bogdo Ola and Songgina in particular were known and

worshipped under the names 'The Lords of the Four Mountains' (*dörben aγula-yin ejed*).[438] In a shamanistic song of invocation recorded in 1928, Tungčingarbo, the spirit of the Bogdo Ola massif, is called upon:

> Accompanied by bears as their travelling companions,
> Setting forth with reddish-grey reindeer,
> They arrived on their
> Thirty-three dun horses.
> Holy Dalha Tungčingarbo,
> You are my refuge and my love,
> The liberation of Umaxum![439]

The spirits of the Bulghan Khangai massif too are invoked as 'Rulers of the Bulghan Khangai' in a song of invocation first recorded in 1957:

> A hui,
> You who have come from the land of Dzagar travelling through Dordzidangui,
> With Dambarai as a crossing-place,
> Rulers of the Bulghan Khangai!
> With a camp in the dry valley of the
> Most famous mountain Budu Dzayirang,
> You who have come descending the valley of the Khusar,
> with a camp on Ulaghan Tolughai,
> With a throne on the Hill of Goats . . . .[440]

Near to the great lake of Khobso Gol in the north-west of Northern Mongolia the shamans worship another mountain-deity, Qan Boγda Dayan Degereki Qayirqan in the form of a rock having human-like appearance. Qayirqan (pronounced 'khärkhan') is a euphemistic term for the holy mountain and means 'the loved, the beautiful'.

> My sovereign, holy mountain Dayan Degereki,
> With a body eighty yards in height,
> With eighty-eight yellow-brown horses!
> My mountain Dayan Degereki Genin-Čimbu!
> With the red Dayičin heroes,
> With Mother Tara Udzardzima,
> With Dalha Wangdud as protective deities!
> My mountain Dayan Degereki,
> You who rise up on the
> South side of the high mountain,
> You who rise up on the

Bank of the Broad River,
You who defend those from the Black Direction,
You who protect those from the White Side,
You who appear like a throne of stone,
You who have the form of a stone monument,
You who are the protection to all men,
You who are the first of all the ten thousand shamans,
You who are the master of thousands of shamans,
My Dayan Degereki, holy mountain . . . ![441]

In this case too the Lamaist church did everything to incorporate this mountain-deity, who is of unambiguously shamanistic origin, into its system and to co-ordinate it with Lamaist gods. Through the prayers however there glimmers the old shamanistic mode of thought:

You who have thirty-three yellow-brown horses,
My grey-haired father, sovereign, you liberator!
My grey-haired father, Khan Dayan,
You who have for passage the Mountain of the Dawn,
You who have for seat the Pass of the Ancestors,
You who have the river Agaru for drink . . . .[442]

The shamanistic origin can be recognized especially clearly where Dayan Degereki is also spoken of as 'Khan, Black Tngri', and where we find:

Khan, Black Tngri
With medicine in your thumb,
With magical healing-power in your index-finger,
With a breast of mineral bronze,
With a hindpart of iron ore,
With the trees of the Khangai as posts to tie up your horses,
With black blood as libation,
You who have drunk the blood of a hundred lamas,
You who have made an ornamental hanging from the skulls of
  a thousand Bandi . . .
With black crows as retinue,
With the young of spotted bats,
You who still do not see a shorn head,
You who see no monk or priest,
You who do not see the yellow and red colour,
You who do not smell the smoke of the incense-offering of
  juniper . . . .[443]

There are pictorial representations too of Dayan Degereki, who

16   Dayan Degereki (devotional print, after Rinchen)

acts as the local deity of North-Western Mongolia, and these are
printed as blockprints on cloth flags.[444] They show Dayan Degereki
as a rider with a Mongolian head-covering and a quiver full of
arrows. The spirit of the southern Bogdo Ola is represented
similarly in temple images, as a rider dressed in white.[445]

The Lamaist church also accepted the embodiments of the 'Lords
of the Four Mountains' into the circle of personages in the mystery-
plays and masked dances (čam, Tibetan 'cham) performed in the
monasteries. The spirit of the mountain of Bayan Jirüke was
represented by the mask of a young man with a yellow face and hair
piled up high like a tower, the spirit of Boydo Ola as a Garuda-bird
with a snake in its beak, the spirit of the Čenggeltü mountain as a
yellow-faced old man with a long moustache, and finally the spirit of
the mountain of Songgina as a dark-skinned old man with thick eye-
brows, tousled hair and a bitter expression on his face.[446] According
to the Mongolian legends the greyish-black old man was once a
mighty shaman who was finally converted after fierce battles with
the adherents of Lamaism.[447]

The total body of material available to us on the Mongol cult of
high places indicates that, despite Lamaistic transformations and

17   Mask of the Lord of Songgina Mountain (after Rinchen)

incorporations, the oldest religious conceptions of the Mongols have survived in the cult of heights, going back to the primary conception of the ancestral spirits and shamanistic spirits which animate and rule the mountains and heights, the rivers and the lakes.

CHRONOLOGICAL TABLE

1206   Enthroning of Činggis Khan as ruler of the Mongols

1207   Mongol troops advance towards Tibet; first contact with Tibetan Buddhism

1247   Prince Godan meets the *Sa skya* Pandita

from 1260 Period of rule of Khubilai Khan as Great Khan; Tibetan Buddhism gains a foothold in Mongolia, missionary activity of the lama *'Phags pa* (1238-80)

1308-12 Reign of Khaishan Külüg as Great Khan; intensive translation of Buddhist scriptures into Mongolian

1368   Collapse of Mongol rule over China; expulsion of the Mongols from China

1431   Buddhist *mantras* printed in China in the Mongolian language

1522-66 Persecutions of Buddhists in China under the Emperor Chia-ching

1557   Birth of Neyiči Toyin among the Torghuts

1573   *bSod nams rgya mtsho* invited to Mongolia by Altan Khan of the Tümet

1576   Journey of *bSod nams rgya mtsho*, the Third Dalai Lama, to Mongolia

1577   Anti-shamanist edicts of Altan Khan; Köke Khota develops into a spiritual and religious centre

1586   Building of the monastery of Erdeni Ĵuu in the Khalkha territory; anti-shamanist edicts of Abadai Khan. Second journey of the Third Dalai Lama to Mongolia; visit among the Kharchin

111

1586	Beginning of another principal centre of translation among the Kharchin
1587	Death of the Third Dalai Lama *bSod nams rgya mtsho*
1588	Birth of the Fourth Dalai Lama in Mongolia; he is the son of a Mongol prince
1599	Birth of *Rab 'byams pa* Caya Pandita
1604	Ligdan Khan of the Chahars begins to reign as Great Khan
1628-9	An editing committee of thirty-five clergy and translators prepares a Mongolian edition of the Kanjur at the wish of Ligdan Khan, in 213 volumes
1629-53	Missionary activity in Eastern Mongolia by Neyiči Toyin; persecution of shamanism
1635	Birth of the First *rJe btsun dam pa* Khutukhtu, called Öndür Gegen
1636-8	Building of the Yellow Temple in Mukden by the Manchu Emperor T'ai-tsung
1642	Birth of the first (Peking) *lCang skya* Khutukhtu, *Ngag dbang blo bzang chos ldan*
1649	Introduction of the West Mongolian script by *Rab 'byams pa* Caya Pandita
1650	Beginning of printing and translation of Buddhist works under the encouragement of the Manchus
1650-2	Translation of 194 mostly canonical scriptures into West Mongolian by Caya Pandita and his collaborators
1653	Death of Neyiči Toyin
1661	Beginning of the reign of the Manchu Emperor K'ang-hsi, well-disposed towards Lamaism
1714	Death of the first (Peking) *lCang skya* Khutukhtu
1717	Birth of the second *lCang skya* Khutukhtu, *Rol pa'i rdo rje*
1717-20	Printing of the Mongolian Kanjur translation in Peking in 108 volumes

1722   Death of the Emperor K'ang-hsi

1722-35   Reign of the Emperor Yung-cheng, particularly favourable to Lamaism

1725   Entry of the second *lCang skya* Khutukhtu, *Rol pa'i rdo rje*, into Peking

1730   Building of the first Lamaist temple on the River Selenga

1734   Entry of the *dGa' ldan* Siregetü Khutukhtu, *Ngag dbang blo bzang bstan pa'i nyi ma,* into Peking

1736   Accession of the Manchu Emperor Ch'ien-lung

1742-9   Translation and printing of the Tanjur in 226 volumes at Imperial command
            Climax of work of translation
            Activity of the Mergen Diyanči lama for a Mongolian national liturgy

1746   Death of the *dGa' ldan* Siregetü Siregetü Khutukhtu

1786   Death of the second (Peking) *lCang skya* Khutukhtu, *Rol pa'i rdo rje*

1787   Birth of the third *lCang skya* Khutukhtu, *Ye shes bstan pa'i rgyal mtshan*

1788   Lamaist missionary activity among the Buryats

1795   Death of the Emperor Ch'ien-lung

1808-20   Anti-shamanist measure among the Buryats

1911   Declaration of independence of Outer Mongolia with the eighth *rJe btsun dam pa* Khutukhtu as Head of State

1924   Formation of the Mongolian People's Republic; prohibition of shamanism in the constitution

NOTES

Chapter 1: Lamaism and folk religion among the Mongols

1 Text No. 12=Heissig, 1961a, XI.
2 Tucci, 1949, vol. 2, p.729 (retranslated from German).
3 Ibid., p.723 (retranslated from German).
4 Text No. 4, edited in Damdinsürüng 1959, translated Heissig, 1953-4.
5 Noted in 1942; Heissig, 1944, pp.64-5.
6 Noted in 1957; Manijab, 1957 pp.10.50-5.
7 Poppe, 1935; Pozdneyev, 1900, p.293; translated into English in Partanen, 1941. Part 5.8.
8 Heissig, 1966c, p.96; Haltod, 1966, pp.76-8.
9 Diószegi, 1963a, pp.267, 374.
10 Heissig, 1953.
11 Sodnam, 1962, pp.73, 91 etc.
12 Rinchen 1959-61, volume 1; Damdinsürüng, 1957a, pp.247-59; Heissig, 1966a, pp.1-53, and the literature cited there.
13 Banzarov, 1846.
14 Heissig, 1954a, pp.128-39.
15 Wright, 1948, p.353.
16 Kiselev, 1951, p.615.
17 Kiselev, 1965, pp.167-73.
18 Egami, 1952, pp.155-267.
19 Mostaert, 1934, pp.1-17.
20 Jahn, 1956, p.88.
21 Heissig, 1966a, pp.165-6.
22 Cf. pp.84ff.

Chapter 2: The shamanism of the Mongols

1 Text No. 23 *(The Secret History of the Mongols)*, para. 216; translated Haenisch, 1937/1962, p.105.
2 Vladimirtsov, 1948, p.61.
3 Text No. 23, para. 103, translated Haenisch, 1937/1962, p.25.
4 Text No. 23, para. 81, translated Haenisch, 1937/1962, p.17.
5 Heissig, 1944.

6 Risch, 1930, pp.62-89.
7 Text No. 26 *(Yüan-shih),* chapter 77, 9v, and chapter 3, 6v; Thiel, 1961, pp.31-2.
8 Serruys, 1945.
9 Text No. 4, 88r; Heissig, 1953, p.494.
10 Mongolian *qosiyun* (Mongolian administrative unit).
11 Text No. 12 (=Heissig 1961a), 28v.
12 Heissig, 1966a, pp.163-8; partial English translation in Heissig, 1953, pp.503-6.
13 Hamada and Mizuno, 1938.
14 Cf. Chapter 5, section 2 below (pp.49ff.).
15 Sandschejew, 1927, p.602.
16 Poppe, 1935, p.107; Partanen, 1941, p.25.
17 Poppe, 1935, p.19 (Chronicle of T. Toboev).
18 Pallas, 1776-1801, volume II, p.347.
19 In the Fürstlich Fürstenbergische Hofbibliothek, Donaueschingen; on Rehmann, cf. Francke, 1951, pp.31-6.
20 Heissig, 1944, pp.48-9. Figure 2; further Sandschejew, 1927.
21 Poppe, 1935, p.95; Partanen, 1941, p.13.
22 Poppe, 1935, p.19 (chronicle of T. Toboev).
23 Ysbrants-Ides, 1704, p.35; Hansen, 1950, p.123.
24 Harlez, 1887, plate VIII.
25 Heissig, 1944, p.65.
26 Torii, 1942, pp.13, 96.
27 Hansen, 1950, p.122. On the question of shamanistic masks see further Diószegi, 1967.
28 Hansen, 1950, p.121.
29 Bodde, 1936, p.78.
30 Diószegi, 1963b, pp.57, 75; Heissig, 1966a, pp.22-3.

Chapter 3: The spread of Lamaism

1 Inaba, 1963, p.108.
2 Yule and Cordier, 1903, vol. I, p.301.
3 Text No. 26, Pen-chi, 33, 7.
4 Text No. 1.
5 Text No. 14; translated I. J. Schmidt, 1829, p.211.
6 Text No. 4, 5v-7r.
7 Cleaves, 1954.
8 Bawden, 1961, p.35.
9 Text No. 12=Heissig 1961a, p.35.
10 Text No. 13=Nasanbaljir, 1960, p.71.
11 Heissig, 1954b.
12 Text No. 17=Huth 1893-96, vol. II, p.225.
13 Text No. 24, p.4.
14 Heissig, 1966d.
15 Heissig, 1962a.

16 Text No. 4, 55v; Heissig, 1953, pp.494-5.
17 Text No. 4, 53v; Heissig, 1953, p.494.
18 Text No. 4, 49r.
19 Heissig, 1953.
20 Text No. 2=Heissig, 1959c, V, 13v.
21 Heissig, 1954a.
22 Text No. 12=Heissig, 1961a.
23 Miller, 1959, p.141.
24 Sagaster, 1960, 1967.
25 Miller, 1959, pp.87-118.
26 Heissig, 1959a, 1965b.

Chapter 4: The Lamaist suppression of shamanism

1 Heissig, 1953, pp.519-24.
2 Text No. 4, 46r-46v.
3 Text No. 4, 53v-54r.
4 Sandschejew, 1927, p.607.
5 Text No. 24, p.17.
6 Poppe, 1935, p.66; Kudryavtsev, 1940, p.138.
7 Poppe, 1935, pp.67, 91-2.
8 Poppe, 1936, p.19 (Chronicle of Lomboceren).
9 Poppe, 1935, p.21 (Chronicle of Toboev).
10 Poppe, 1935, p.32.
11 Ibid., p.34.
12 Loc.cit.
13 Text No. 4, 8v.
14 Text No. 24, p.5.
15 Weber, 1923, vol. II, p.254.
16 Hoffmann, 1950, pp.222-9.
17 Text No. 25.
18 Text No. 4, 41r.
19 Text No. 4, 75v.
20 Text No. 4, 83v.
21 Pozdneyev, 1887, pp.202-33. Translated in Unkrig, 1927.
22 Lessing, 1935, p.143.
23 Nebesky-Wojkowitz, 1956, p.411.
24 Hoffmann, 1950, p.194.
25 Schröder, 1952, pp. 18ff.
26 Heissig, 1944.
27 Text No. 10, VII, No. 75.
28 Heissig, 1963a, pp.557-90.
29 Heissig, 1954a, pp.151-4.
30 Heissig, 1966a, pp.8-9, Nos. XXVIII, XLII, XXIII.
31 Heissig, 1954a, No. 159.
32 Poppe, 1932a, p.185.
33 Heissig, 1944.

34 Heissig, 1966c.
35 Sodnam, 1962.

Chapter 5: The Mongolian folk religion and its pantheon

1 Heissig, 1966a, pp.1-53.
2 Mostaert, 1957a.
3 Poppe, 1925, p.140.
4 Text No. 21, II, 9r.
5 Mostaert, 1962, p.212; Heissig, 1966a, pp.16ff.
6 Jimba, 1958, pp.98-102; Damdinsürüng, 1957a, pp.247-59.
7 Poppe, 1957, in particular pp. 67-76; Mostaert and Cleaves, 1962, pp. 18-22.
8 Haenisch, 1941, pp.118, 145.
9 Ibid., p.31.
10 Ibid., p.34.
11 van den Wyngaert, 1929, p.36.
12 Poppe 1957, p.69; Bang-Kaup, p.247.
13 Thiel, 1961, p.31.
14 Text No. 27; Poppe, 1932a, p.161.
15 Rinchen, 1959-61, No. I.
16 Heissig, 1966a, No. I.
17 Rinchen, 1959-61, No. XXII, p.43.
18 Heissig, 1966a, No. III.
19 Rinchen, 1959-61, No. XIII, p.27; Poppe, 1932a, p.175.
20 Rinchen, 1959-61, No. XXVIII, p.54.
21 Ibid., No. XXXVI, p.75.
22 Heissig, 1966a, No. II, p.58.
23 Ibid., p.60.
24 Loc.cit.
25 Poppe, 1932a, p.165 (Text No. 28).
26 Cf. p.75.
27 Heissig, 1966a, No. IV and others.
28 Rinchen, 1959-61, No. I, p.1; No. III, p.4.
29 Heissig, 1966a, No. LXVI, p.227.
30 Ibid., No. VI, p.74; Rinchen, 1959-61, pp.98, 101.
31 Heissig, 1966a, No. XI, p.93.
32 Mostaert, 1962, p.202; Heissig, 1966a, No. XI, p.93.
33 Banzarov, 1955, p.65; W. Schmidt, 1952, vol. X, pp.63-6.
34 Mostaert, 1957b.
35 Sodnam, 1962, pp.71, 87, song of a shaman and a shamaness from the Old Bargha region. Partanen, 1941, part 5, 8.
36 Text No. 5; Pozdneyev, 1900, pp.293-311. English translation in Partanen 1941, part 5. Poppe, 1935.
37 Rinchen, 1959-61, I, pp.9, 22, 31.
38 Ibid., p.36; Heissig, 1966a, No. IX.
39 Banzarov, 1955, p.76.
40 Rinchen, 1959-61, p.73.

41 Text No. 29, 13v.
42 Rinchen, 1959-61, p.49.
43 Heissing, 1966a, p.90.
44 Text No. 7, p.196.
45 Heissig, 1966a, pp.60, 74; Rinchen, 1959-61, p.14.
46 Rinchen, 1959-61, pp.35, 55, 86.
47 Rinchen, 1959-61, pp.49, 35; Damdinsürüng 1959, p.197; Heissig, 1966a, p.228.
48 Jangča böge, Heissig, 1944, Wančanmayadaγ böge, cf. Manijab, 1957, p.10; Heissig, 1966c, pp.91-5.
49 Heissig, 1944.
50 Heissig, 1966c, pp.91-5.
51 Rinchen, 1959-61, I, p.35; Heissig, 1968b, p.268.
52 Heissig, 1966c, pp.91-5.
53 Banzarov, 1846, reprinted in Banzarov, 1955.
54 Rinchen, 1959-61, p.35.
55 Poppe, 1932a, pp.158, 159.
56 Poppe, 1932a, pp.158, 159, 162.
57 Partanen, 1941, p.8.
58 Loc.cit.
59 Poppe, 1932a, p.162.
60 Ibid., p.161.
61 Ibid., p.158.
62 Partanen, 1941, p.9; Poppe, 1932a, p.159; Rinchen, 1959-61, I, p.56.
63 Partanen, 1941, p.9.
64 Rinchen, 1959-61, I, p.34.
65 Poppe, 1932a, pp.159-60.
66 Partanen, 1941, p.8.
67 Poppe, 1932a, p.162.
68 Ibid., p.163.
69 Loc.cit.
70 Ibid., pp.164-5.
71 Ibid., p.162.
72 Rinchen, 1959-61, I, p.34.
73 Heissig, 1966a, p.227.
74 Rinchen, 1959-61, I, p.5.
75 Ibid., I, p.48.
76 Poppe, 1932a, p.162.
77 Rinchen, 1959-61, I, p.34.
78 Ibid., I, p.45.
79 Poppe, 1932a, p.162.
80 Rinchen, 1959-61, I, p.2.
81 Ibid., I, p.33.
82 Ibid., I, p.6.
83 Ibid., I, p.71.
84 Ibid., I, p.98.
85 Poppe, 1932a, p.160; Rinchen, 1959-61, I, pp.54, 57; Heissig, 1966a, p.227.

86   Poppe, 1932a, p.170.
87   Heissig, 1966a, p.227, where *alba* for lit. *aliba*; Poppe, 1932a, p.170.
88   On this see also Poppe, 1932a.
89   Poppe, 1932a, p.163.
90   Rinchen 1959-61, pp.35, 55, 86; Heissig, 1966a, p.227; Poppe, 1932a, pp.171, 173.
91   Rinchen, 1959-61, p.34; Poppe, 1932a, p.171.
92   Rinchen, 1959-61, I, p.34.
93   Partanen, 1941, p.9; Heissig, 1953, p.507.
94   Partanen, 1941, p.9.
95   Poppe, 1932a, p.155.
96   Ibid., pp.155-6.
97   Rinchen, 1959-61, I, p.40; Dandinsürüng, 1959, p.122.
98   Rinchen, 1959-61, I, p.42.
99   Ibid., I, p.41.
100 Loc.cit.
101 Mostaert, 1949, p.503.
102 Sandschejew, 1927, p.600.
103 Rinchen, 1959-61, I, p.35.
104 Cf. p.50.
105 Partanen, 1941, p.8.
106 Rinchen, 1959-61, I, p.35.
107 Poppe, 1932a, p.164.
108 Loc.cit.
109 Loc.cit.
110 Loc.cit.
111 Songs of invocation of East Mongolian shamans Jangča and Wančan-mayaḍaγ (Heissig, 1944, p.58, 1966c, p.84); song of Aru Khorchin shaman (Sodnam, 162, pp.101-2).
112 Heissig, 1966c, p.85.
113 Heissig, 1944, p.59; 1966c, pp.85, 98.
114 Partanen, 1941, p.9; Damdinsürüng, 1959, No. 13; Heissig, 1966a, p.49.
115 Damdinsürüng, p.129.
116 Rinchen, 1959-61, pp.34, 35, 55, 86; Poppe, 1932a, p.171.
117 Poppe, 1932b, pp.156-9; 1955, pp.264-9.
118 Haltod, 1966, p.77.
119 Damdinsürüng, 1959, p.129.
120 Loc.cit.
121 Rinchen, 1959-61, II, pp. 10, 20, 40, 44, 70, 77, 78; Haltod, 1966, p.79.
122 Sodnam, 1962, p.86.
123 Heissig, 1966c, table, p.91.
124 Manijab, 1957, p.10; Heissig, 1966c, p.84.
125 Poppe, 1932a, p.158.
126 Partanen, 1941, pp.9-10.
127 Damdinsürüng, 1959, p.129.
128 Heissig, 1966a, pp.163-76; 1953, pp.503-6.
129 Text No. 26, chapter 77; Thiel, 1961, p.31.

130 Potanin, 1893, I, pp.121-9; Lüdtke, 1927; Lattimore, 1941, pp.39-60; Rinchen, 1959.
131 Dylykov, 1958, pp.235-9.
132 Text No. 18, III, 1904-6.
133 Heissig, 1950a, pp.615-17.
134 Rinchen, 1959-61, I, IX; Sagaster, 1966.
135 Mostaert, 1957c, p.535.
136 Sugiyama, 1940, pp.64-77.
137 Rinchen, 1959-61, I, p.11; Heissig, 1966a, p.105.
138 Sugiyama, 1940, pp.64-77.
139 Rinchen, 1959-61, I, pp.63-5, 67-9, 94.
140 Ibid., I, p.91.
141 Ibid., I, pp.63, 67.
142 Ibid., I, p.94.
143 Ibid., I, p.96.
144 Text No. 8; Damdinsürüng, 1959, pp.60-73; translation into German in Heissig, 1962b.
145 Text No. 7.
146 Rinchen, 1959-61, I, p.95.
147 Ibid., I, p.96.
148 Loc.cit
149 Weekly newspaper *Köke Tuγ*, New Year 1940.
150 Rinchen, 1959-61, I, pp.84-5; Dylykov, 1959.
151 Rinchen, 1959-61, I, p.96.
152 Ibid., I, p.97.
153 Ibid., I, p.98.
154 Lüdtke, 1927, p.127.
155 Heissig, 1966a, p.8, note 3.
156 Rinchen, 1959-61, I, p.66.
157 Heissig, 1966a, pp.30, 151-3.
158 Ibid., p.152.
159 Cf. pp.93ff.
160 Heissig, 1966a, p.152.
161 Rinchen, 1959-61, I, p.66.
162 Zhamtsarano, 1936, pp.70-8; translated in Löwenthal, 1955, pp.50-5.
163 Heissig, 1959a, pp.17-26.
164 Zhamtsarano, 1936, p.75 (Löwenthal 1955, p.53); Heissig, 1959a, facsimilia 14-15.
165 Cf. Mostaert, 1935, p.335.
166 Yule and Cordier, 1903, I, p.300.
167 Mostaert, 1935, p.335.
168 Text No. 19, an address called *Körku nekekü öndür ǰalaγu* in a ritual handbook from Ordos, in the possession of J. V. Hecken of Louvain. Cf. *Zentralasiatische Studien*, vol. 2 (1968).
169 Text No. 6, p.69 of 1941 Kalgan edition; cf. Heissig, 1946, pp.60-1.
170 *gegüü-yin sime öčig sačuli-yi.*
171 Rinchen, 1959-61, I, p.33.
172 Heissig, 1966a, No. XLVII.

173 Ibid., No. XLVIII.
174 Ibid., No. LV; English translation in Heissig, 1950b, p.162.
175 Text No. 38, p.68. Concerning this text cf. Heissig, 1965a, p.165.
176. Heissig, 1966, No. XLIII.
177 Text No. 6, p.32 of 1941 Kalgan edition; Mostaert and Cleaves, 1959, part IV, p.36; Heissig, 1946, p.51.
178 Rinchen, 1959-61, No. XXV, pp.47-8.
179 Heissig, 1962b, p.51.
180 Horloo, 1960, pp.89-92.
181 Text No. 15; Mongolian tradition from Ordos, Mostaert, 1937, p.131 and 1949, p.188.
182 Text No. 26.
183 Heissig, 1966a, Nos. LVIII and LIX.
184 Ibid., No. XXXV.
185 Ibid., No. LX.
186 Text No. 38, p.101.
187 Heissig, 1959a.
188 Poppe, 1925, p.212.
189 Ibid., p.140; Mostaert, 1962, pp.212.
190 The oldest European description of this ceremony, with translation of a fire-hymn, in Pallas 1776-1801, vol. II, pp.327-33; further Poppe, 1925, pp.140-5; Mostaert, 1962, pp.211-3.
191 Heissig, 1966a, pp.11-18.
192 Mostaert, 1962, p.213.
193 Heissig, 1966a, p.256.
194 Mostaert, 1962, p.213; 1937, pp.461-2.
195 Mostaert, 1962, p.213; 1956, p.276.
196 Poppe, 1925, p.132.
197 On this already Banzarov, 1955, p.34; Poppe, 1932a, p.133.
198 Rinchen, 1959-61, I, p.30.
199 Poppe, 1925, p.135.
200 Rinchen, 1959-61, I, p.30.
201 Heissig, 1966a, p.87.
202 Poppe, 1925, p.135.
203 Heissig, 1966a, p.72.
204 Damdinsürüng, 1959, p.111; Poppe, 1925, p.136; Rinchen, 1959-61, I, p.15; Heissig 1966a, p.66.
205 Rinchen, 1959-61, I, p.14; Heissig, 1966a, pp.66, 69, 74, 77.
206 Mostaert, 1962, pp.194, 197; Heissig, 1966a, p.74; Poppe, 1925, p.136.
207 Heissig, 1966a, p.66; Mostaert, 1962, p.194.
208 Mostaert, 1962, pp.194, 219; Heissig, 1966a, pp.66ff.
209 West Mongolian; Heissig, 1966a, p.95.
210 Heissig, 1966a, p.113; Bawden, 1963.
211 Heissig, 1966a, p.72.
212 Poppe, 1925.
213 Rinchen, 1959-61, pp.17, 33.
214 Poppe, 1932a, p.137; Rinchen, 1959-61, I, p.9.

215 Rinchen, 1959-61, I, p.9.
216 Poppe, 1925, p.138.
217 Rinchen, 1959-61, I, p.9.
218 Damdinsürüng, 1959, p.112.
219 Rinchen, 1959-61, I, p.9.
220 Heissig, 1966a, p.88; Damdinsürüng, 1959, p.112.
221 Heissig, 1966a, p.82; Rinchen, 1959-61, I, p.23.
222 Heissig, 1966a, p.80.
223 Vladimirtsov, 1924, pp.119-21.
224 Rinchen, 1959-61, I, p.19.
225 Ibid., I, p.27; Poppe, 1925, p.138.
226 Poppe, 1925, p.135.
227 Rinchen, 1959-61, I, p.18; Poppe, 1925, p.135.
228 Mostaert, 1962, pp.195, 198; Poppe, 1932a, p.183; Poppe, 1925, p.135.
229 Heissig, 1966a, pp.103-4.
230 Rinchen, 1959-61, p.10; Heissig, 1966a, pp.103-4.
231 Poppe, 1932a, p.180; 1925, p.133.
232 Poppe, 1925, p.34.
233 Heissig, 1966a, p.13.
234 Ibid., p.119.
235 Ibid., p.127.
236 Text No. 21, II, 9v: *Zentralasiatische Studien,* vol. 2 (1968).
237 Poppe, 1925, p.141.
238 Heissig, 1966a, p.95, note 4; Poppe, 1925, p.142.
239 Heissig, 1966a, p.88.
240 Rinchen, 1959-61, I, p.33.
241 Heissig, 1966a, p.15.
242 Poppe, 1925, p.142.
243 Heissig, 1966a, pp.88-9; Poppe, 1925, pp.139-40.
244 Hummel, 1960.
245 Rock, 1952, I, p.79.
246 Lessing, 1942, p.36.
247 W. A. Unkrig in Filchner, 1933, note 1388; Pozdneyev, 1887, pp.83-4.
248 Heissig, 1963b, pp.57-63, 95-9 etc.
249 Heissig, 1966a, Nos XIX, XX; Poppe, 1932a, p.187.
250 Heissig, 1966a, No. XXI; Pozdneyev, 1887, p.84, note 1.
251 Diószegi, 1963b, pp.57, 75.
252 Ibid., p.57: *tayay* or *morin toluyaitu tayay.*
253 Mostaert, 1957a, p.110; Poppe, 1935, p.94.
254 Mostaert, 1957a, p.112.
255 *Secret History of the Mongols* (Text No. 23), translated by Haenisch 1941, p.216.
256 Heissig, 1966a, p.19.
257 Ibid., p.18.
258 Poppe, 1932a, p.187; Mostaert, 1957a, p.109.
259 Heissig, 1966a, No. XXI; Pozdneyev, 1887, pp.85-6.
260 Text No. 30; Heissig, 1966a, p.79; Pozdneyev, 1887, p.86.
261 Edited by Damdinsürüng, 1959, pp.221-7; Potanin, 1881-3, pp.310-20.

262 Text No. 31, cf. Heissig, 1966a, p.22.
263 Heissig, 1966a, No. XXIII; translation Mostaert, 1957a, pp.116-17.
264 *Mergen süme-yin ǧam-un üye jerge-yi kerkijü bayičayaqu temdeg bičig almas erke* (Text No.11, volume III, cf. Heissig 1954a, p.153, No. 22).
265 Heissig, 1966a, No. XXI; Pozdneyev, 1887, p.84.
266 Heissig, 1966a, No. XIX.
267 Ibid., Nos XX, XXI; Pozdneyev, 1887, p.84.
268 Heissig, 1966a, No. XX.
269 Ibid., Nos XX, XXI.
270 Mostaert, 1957a, pp.116-17.
271 Heissig, 1966a, No. XIX.
272 Ibid., No. XXII.
273 Poppe, 1935, p.94; Mostaert, 1957a, p.109.
274 Mostaert, 1957a, p.112.
275 Heissig, 1966a, No. XX.
276 Mostaert, 1957a, p.112.
277 Mongolian *Jimis-tü* or *Jimislig*.
278 Mostaert, 1957a, p.110.
279 Mostaert, 1957a, p.111; Hummel, 1960, p.203.
280 Heissig, 1966a, plate XV.
281 Hummel, 1960, pp.204-6.
282 Heissig, 1954a, p.153, No. 162, 22.
283 Lüdtke, 1927, pp. 95, 115.
284 Rinchen, 1959-61, I, p.86.
285 Banzarov, 1846, p.73.
286 Laufer, 1907.
287 Damdinsürüng, 1959, p.131.
288 Lüdtke, 1927, p.115.
289 Damdinsürüng, 1959, p.131.
290 Loc.cit.
291 Poppe, 1932a, p.184.
292 Damdinsürüng, 1959, p.134.
293 Ibid., p.135.
294 Heissig, 1966d, p.54.
295 Damdinsürüng, 1959, pp.135-6.
296 Mándoki, 1963.
297 Hoffmann, 1950, p.172; Heissig, 1964.
298 Nebesky-Wojkowitz, 1956, pp.318-40.
299 Text No. 23, para. 249; cf. Haenisch, 1941, p.126 and 1937-9, p.85 (=1962, p.85).
300 Vocabulary to Haenisch, 1937-9, p.137 (=1962, p.137).
301 Cf. p.59.
302 Zhamtsarano, 1913, p.46.
303 Lattimore, in *Pacific Affairs*.
304 Mostaert, 1957c, p.535.
305 Rinchen, 1959-61, I, No. XXXV, pp.72-3.
306 Ibid., I, No. XXXII, p.66.
307 Heissig, 1966a, No. XXXIII, p.162.

308 Rinchen, 1959-61, I, No. XXXVII, p.76.
309 Ibid., No. XXXXV, p.101.
310 Cf. the two prayers for the *sülde* of Sayang Sečen and of his great-grandfather, Mostaert, 1957c, pp.544-66.
311 Rinchen, 1959-61, No. XXXVI, p.74.
312 Banzarov *(Chernaya vyera)*, 1955, p.80; W. Schmidt, 1952, vol. X, p.79.
313 Rinchen, 1959-61, I, No. XXV, p.49.
314 Ibid., I, No. XXIII, p.45.
315 Ibid., I, No. XXXVII, p.83.
316 Heissig, 1966a, No. XXXIII, pp.162-3; 1959b, pp.44-5.
317 Rinchen, 1959-61, No. XXXVIII, p.83.
318 Loc.cit.
319 Poppe, 1932a, pp.168-9; Heissig, 1954a, No. 161.
320 Summary in Nebesky-Wojkowitz, 1956, pp.336-8.
321 Heissig, 1964, pp.200-2.
322 Text No. 11, volume N/12, 13; cf. Banzarov, 1955, p.80; W. Schmidt, 1952, vol. X, p.79.
323 Nebesky-Wojkowitz, 1956, p.336.
324 Heissig, 1966a, No. XXXII, p.102; cf. Heissig, 1964, pp. 196-200; Rinchen, 1959-61, I, No. XXXVIII, p.33.
325 Dylykov, 1958, pp.235-75; Rumyantsev in footnote 112 to Banzarov, 1955, p.273.
326 Banzarov *(Chernaya vyera)*, 1955, p.77 (and W. Schmidt, 1952, vol. X, p.77, following Banzarov); Text No. 35 (Heissig, 1961b, No. 8); Mongolian text ed. Damdinsürüng, 1959, p.186; English translation Bawden, 1967, pp. 60-2.
327 Ed. Damdinsürüng, 1959, p.187.
328 Bergmann, 1804-5, pp.70, 54.
329 Text No. 20, VI, 54; cf. Heissig, 1959b, pp.47-8.
330 Consten, 1919-20, II, p.214; Maiskii, 1921, pp.255-6; Heissig, 1959b, pp.47-50.
331 Rinchen 1951-3, vol. II, p.284; translated in Heissig, 1959b, pp.49-50.
332 Heissig, 1966a, No. XXXIII, pp.159-63.
333 Cf. p.87.
334 Rinchen, 1958a, p.33.
335 Text No. 32, cf. Heissig, 1961b, No. 81; Text No. 9, volume 5.
336 Text No. 10, Volume 7, No. 75.
337 Cf. Heissig, 1964, p.202.
338 Damdinsürüng, 1959, p.129.
339 Cf. p.90.
340 Heissig, 1966a, No. XXXI, p.157; cf. also Heissig, 1964, pp.194-5.
341 Heissig, 1966a, No. XXVII, p.148; No. XXV, p.143.
342 Incense offering for Geser Khan. Rinchen, 1958a, p.28.
343 Loc.cit.
344 Ibid., pp.29-30.
345 Heissig, 1966a, No. XXVII, p.150.
346 Ibid., No. XXVII, p.149.
347 Rinchen, 1958a, p.28.

348 Heissig, 1966a, No. XXVII, p.149.
349 Ibid., No. XXIV, p.141.
350 Cf. Kler, 1957; Mostaert, 1956, pp.289-90.
351 Rinchen, 1958a, p.30.
352 Heissig, 1966a, No. XXVII, p.146.
353 Rinchen, 1958a, p.32.
354 Heissig, 1966a, No. XXIV, p.140.
355 Rinchen, 1958a, p.28.
356 Heissig, 1966a, No. XXV, p.142.
357 Ibid., No. XXVII, p.146.
358 Ibid., No. XXIV, p. 143.
359 Rinchen, 1958a, pp.37-8.
360 Heissig, 1966a, No. XXV, p.142.
361 Rinchen, 1958a, pp.26-7.
362 Heissig, 1966a, No. XXIV, pp.140-1.
363 Rinchen 1958a, pp.30-1.
364 Cf. p.90.
365 Tucci, 1949, vol. II, pp.571-4, 735-6.
366 Rinchen, 1958a, p.29; cf. further Damdinsürüng, 1955, p.54.
367 Rinchen, 1958a, p.28.
368 Cf. p.90; Rinchen, 1958a, p.33.
369 Nebesky-Wojkowitz, 1956, p.318; Rinchen, 1958a, p.6.
370 Nebesky-Wojkowitz, 1956, p.462.
371 Ibid., pp.281, 309 etc.
372 Roerich, 1942, p.285; Stein, 1959, plates III and IV.
373 Heissig, 1966a, p.28, No. XXIV, p.141.
374 Ibid., p.28; No. XXVI, p.145; No. XXVII, p.147.
375 Ibid., p.29; No. XXV, p.143; No. XXVI, p.145; No. XXVII.
376 Ibid., No. XXIV, p.141.
377 Ibid., No. XXV, p.143.
378 Ibid., No. XXIV, p.141.
379 Rinchen, 1958a, p.27.
380 Text No. 3, II, 5; Text No. 36, 50; Heissig, 1962b, p.94.
381 Heissig, 1966a, No. XXVII, p.149.
382 Rinchen, 1960.
383 Heissig, 1966a, pp.48-9; Ms.Mong. 401, Royal Library, Copenhagen; *Corpus Scriptorum Mongolorum* IX, fasc. 4a, Ulanbator, 1960, p.500.
384 Heissig, 1966a, No. XXXIV, pp.163-8.
385 Heissig, 1953, p. 501.
386 Heissig, 1966a, p.165.
387 Roerich, 1942.
388 Heissig, 1954a, No. 35.
389 Lessing, 1942, I, p.97.
390 Roerich, 1942, p.306; Giles, 1912, p.802.
391 Fuchs, 1936, pp.40, 124.
392 Rinchen, 1958a, pp.17-20.
393 Heissig, 1954a, No. 159.
394 Ms., Royal Library, Copenhagen, 2 fols.

395 Ms., Royal Library, Copenhagen, 9 fols.
396 Roerich, 1942, p.306.
397 Damdinsürüng 1955, pp.57-62; Pozdneyev, 1896-8, vol. II.
398 *Erdeni-yin erike* (by Galdan), Text No. 13, for 1787.
399 Pozdneyev 1896-8, pp.175-6.
400 Heissig, 1954a, No. 206.
401 Ms.Mong. 171, Royal Library, Copenhagen; Bischoff 1961, pp.306-10.
402 Text No. 16 from the year Chia-ch'ing 13; cf. Rinchen, 1958a, pp.39-50.
403 Nebesky-Wojkowitz, 1956, p.462.
404 Rinchen, 1958a, pp.13-17.
405 Heissig, 1966a, No. XXIV, p.140.
406 Damdinsürüng, 1955, p.54.
407 Heissig, 1944, p.64.
408 Heissig, 1955, pp.133-5.
409 Moule and Pelliot, 1938, p.170; Mostaert, 1957b.
410 Banzarov, 1846, pp.16-17 (=1955, p.66).
411 Becquet and Hambis, 1965, pp.40, 146.
412 Heissig, 1966a, pp.74-5.
413 Heissig, 1966d, pp.70-1.
414 Becquet and Hambis, 1965, p.38; Yule and Cordier, 1903, p.257.
415 Hattori, 1940, pp.264-6.
416 Kazakevich, 1934, p.6.
417 Text No. 23, ed. Haenisch, 1962, p.18, para. 103.
418 Ibid.; Poucha, 1956, p.178.
419 Heissig, 1966a, p.164; Heissig, 1953, p.504.
420 Poucha, 1956, p.176.
421 Hamada and Mizuno, 1938.
422 Pallas, 1776-1801, II, p.215.
423 Text No. 22, 64r.
424 Banzarov, 1955, pp.65-72; W. Schmidt, 1952, vol. X, pp.67-9.
425 Heissig, 1954a, No. 162.
426 Text No. 33, 1r; Bawden, 1958, p.27.
427 Nebesky-Wojkowitz, 1956, pp.198, 291-8. For the later distinctions between dragons and water-spirits in the Buddhist vocabularies of the eighteenth century, cf. Bischoff 1961, p.309.
428 Text No. 38, 1r (Heissig, 1954a, No. 126); Bawden, 1958, p.28.
429 Text No. 33, 14v.
430 Ibid., 14v-15r; Bawden, 1958, pp.38-9.
431 Poppe, 1932a, pp. 184-5.
432 Heissig, 1966a, p.31.
433 Heissig, 1966a, p.154.
434 Ibid., p.156.
435 Ibid., p.155.
436 Ibid., p.156.
437 Schubert, 1966.
438 Rinchen, 1958b, p.444.
439 Translated by Rinchen, 1958b, p.444.
440 Haltod, 1966, pp.77-8.

441 Damdinsürüng, 1959, p.128.
442 Rinchen, 1955, pp.14-15.
443 Damdinsürüng, 1959, p.130.
444 Rinchen, 1955, p.13.
445 Rinchen, 1958b, p.444.
446 Ibid., pp.444-8.
447 Ibid., p.448; Forman and Rintschen, 1967, pp.116-19.

BIBLIOGRAPHY

I Manuscripts, blockprints, etc. in Mongolian, Tibetan, Chinese

1. *Altan erike*, Mongolian chronicle by Ārya Paṇḍita *mkhan po* of the Khalkhas (1817). Mss. in Royal Library, Copenhagen.
2. *Altan kürdün mingɣan gegesütü bičig*, Mongolian chronicle by Siregetü Guosi Dharma (1739). Edited by Heissig (1959c).
3. *Arban jüg-ün ejen geser qaɣan-u tuɣuji*. Peking, 1956.
4. *Boɣda neyiči toyin ḍalai mañjušryi yin domoɣ* by Prajñasagara (1739). Peking blockprint. Cf. Damdinsürüng (1959), Heissig (1953-4).
5. *Böge-yin mörgül-ün učira*. Cf. Pozdneyev (1900), Partanen (1941).
6. *Bolur erike*, Mongolian chronicle by Rasipungsuɣ (1774-5). Kalgan edition, 1941 (Chahar Mongol Library of Editions and Translations). Edited by Heissig (1946), Mostaert and Cleaves (1959).
7. *Činggis qaɣan-u cadig*. Peking, Mongɣol bičig-ün qoriya (Mongol Book Office), 1925.
8. *Činggis qaman-u quyar ere-yin jayal-un tuɣuji*.
9. *Collected Works* of the Fifth Dalai Lama.
10. *Collected Works* of the first (Peking) *lCang skya* Khutukhtu, *Ngag dbang blo bzang chos ldan*.
11. *Collected Works of* Mergen Diyanči-yin gegen.
12. *Erdeni-yin erike*, Mongolian chronicle by Isibalden (1835). Edited by Heissig (1961a).
13. *Erdeni-yin erike*, Mongolian chronicle by Tayiji Galden (1859). Edited by Nasanbaljir (1960).
14. *Erdeni-yin tobci*, Mongolian chronicle by Saɣang Sečen (1662). Edited by J. Schmidt (1829), Mostaert and Cleaves (1956).
15. *Erten-ü caɣ-un bolur toli kemekü teüke* (?1880). Mss. from Chahar, Royal Library, Copenhagen.
16. *Geser boɣda-yin tölge*.
17. *Hor chos 'byung* by *'Jigs med rig pa'i rdo rje*. Edited and translated by Huth (1893-6).
18. *Köke sudur* by Injanasi. Peking edition, 1959.
19. *Körke nekekü boro öndür jalaqu*. Ms., Louvain.
20. *Man-chou shih-lu*.
21. *Mongɣol kümün-ü ekilen ürejigsen ɣajar yabuju iregsen jang aɣali-yin bičig* by Lubsangcondan. Ms., Foreign Language University, Tokyo.

128

22. *Mongɣol-un ǰang aɣali-yi tobčilan debter* by Lubsangcondan. Ms.
23. *Mongɣol-un niɣucan tobčiya* (Yüan ch'ao pi-shih, Secret History of the Mongols). Haenisch (1937-9, 1948, 1962), Poucha (1956).
24. Mongolian biography of Caya Pandita. *Corpus Scriptorum Mongolorum* vol. 5, fasc. 2, Ulanbator 1959.
25. *Sungdui (Tarnis-un quriyangɣui)*. Peking blockprint, 1707.
26. *Yüan shih* (History of the Mongol Dynasty).
27. Ms. Leningrad C 148.
28. Ms. Leningrad C 234.
29. Ms., Musée Guimet, Paris, No. 46, 346.
30. Ms. Or. Oct. 422-8, Westdeutsche Staatsbibliothek, Marburg.
31. Ms. L4, New Delhi.
32. Ms. Or. Fol. 1593-A, Westdeutsche Staatsbibliothek, Marburg.
33. *Oboɣa takiqu ǰang üile.*
34. *Oboɣa bosqaqu yosun.*
35. *Dörbön oyirad mongɣoli daruqsan tuži.* Msc. Dresden Eb.404^i, cf. Heissig (1961b), No. 8.
36. Ms. Scheut Mong. 45.
37. Ms. Mong. 401, Royal Library, Copenhagen.
38. *Irügel maytaɣal.* (Collection of blessing-formulae and praise-formulae.) Öbör mongɣol-un arad-un keblel-ün qoriya. Köke Khots 1959. Cf. Heissig (1965a), pp.165-8.

II Other books and articles

Aoki, T. (1952), 'Mokōjin ni okeru hi to ro' (Fire and hearth among the Mongols), *Kōchi daigaku gakujutsu kenkyū hōkoku* (Research reports of the Kochi University), I(17).

Bang-Kaup, W., *Der komanische Marienpsalter nebst seiner Quelle herausgegeben.*

Banzarov, D. (1846), *Chernaya vyera ili shamanstvo u mongolov,* first edition, Kazan (second edition in Banzarov, 1955).

Banzarov, D. (1955), *Sobranie sochinenii* (Collected Works), edited by G. D. Sanzheyev, Moscow.

Bawden, C. R. (1958), 'Two Mongol texts concerning Obo-worship', *Oriens Extremus,* vol. 5, no. 1, pp.23-41.

Bawden, C. R. (1961), *The Jebtsundamba Khutukhtus of Urga.* Text, translation and notes (Asiatische Forschungen, Bd.9), Wiesbaden.

Bawden, C. R. (1963), 'Mongol notes, I,' *Central Asiatic Journal,* vol. 8 (December 1963), pp.281-303.

Bawden, C. R. (1967), 'The tale of Ubashi Khungtaiji of the Mongols', *New Orient,* vol. 6, pp.60-2.

Becquet, J. and Hambis, L. (1965), *Giovanni da Pian del Carpine. Histoire des Mongols, traduit et annotté,* Paris.

Bergmann, B. F. B. von (1804-5), *Nomadische Streifereien unter den Kalmüken in den Jahren 1802 und 1803,* Riga.

Bischoff, F. A. (1961), 'Eine buddhistische Wiedergabe christlicher Bräuche', *Monumenta Serica,* vol. 20, pp.282-310.

Bodde, D. (1963), *Annual Customs and Festivals in Peking*, as recorded in the Yen-ching Sui-shih-chi by Tun Li-ch'en; translated and annotated, Peiping (second, revised edition, Hong Kong, 1965).

Cleaves, F. W. (1954), 'A medical practice of the Mongols in the Thirteenth Century', *Harvard Journal of Asiatic Studies*, vol. 17, pp.428-44.

Consten, H. (1919-20), *Weideplätze der Mongolen im reiche der Chalcha*, Berlin (2 vol.).

Dalai, C. (1959), 'Mongolyn böögijn mörgölijn tovč tüüh', *Studia Ethnographica* (Ulan Bator, Institutum Historiae) I/5.

Damdinsürüng, C. (1955), 'Mongol'skii epos o Geser-Khane', *Archiv Orientalni* (Prague), vol. 23, pp.52-62.

Damdinsürüng, C. (1957a), *Mongyol-un uran jokiyal-un teüke*, Mukden.

Damdinsürüng, C. (1957b), *Istoricheskie korni Geseriady*, Moscow.

Damdinsürüng, C. (1959), Mongol texts edited in *Corpus Scriptorum Mongolorum* (Ulan Bator, Institute of Language and Literature), vol. 14.

Diószegi, V. (ed.) (1963a), *Glaubenswelt und Folklore der sibirischen Völker*, Budapest.

Diószegi, V. (1963b), 'Ethnogenic aspects of Darkhat shamanism', *Acta Orientalia Academiae Scientiarum Hungaricae*, vol. 16, pp.55-81.

Diószegi, V. (1967), 'The origins of the Evenki "shaman-mask"', *Acta Orientalia Academiae Scientiarum Hungaricae*, vol. 20, pp.171-201.

Dylykov, S. D. (1958), *Edzhen-Khoro*, in *Filologiya, Istoriya Mongolskikh narodov* (Pamyati akademika Borisa Yakovlevicha Vladimirtsova), Moscow.

Egami, N. (1952), 'Olon-sume et la decouverte de l'église catholique romaine de Jean de Montecorvino', *Journal Asiatique*, vol. 240, fasc. 2, pp. 155-67.

Filchner, W. (1933), *Kumbum Dschamba Ling, das Kloster der hunderttausend Bilder Maitreyas*, Leipzig.

Forman, W. and Rintschen, B. (1967), *Lamaistische Tanzmasken; der Erlik-Tsam in der Mongolei*, Leipzig.

Franke, H. (1951), 'Unveröffentlichte Reiseberichte und Materialen über Sibirien, die Mongolei und China', *Sinologica*, vol. 3, no. 1, pp.31-6.

Fuchs, W. (1946), *Beiträge zur Mandjurischen Bibliographie und Literatur*, Tokyo (Supplement der *Mitteilungen der Deutschen Gesellschaft für Natur- und Volkerkunde Ostasiens*).

Gaadamba, M. and Cerensodnom, D. (1967), 'Mongol ardyn aman zohiolyn deež bičig', *Studia Folclorica* (Ulan Bator, Institute of Language and Literature), vol. 5, fasc. 1.

Giles, H. A. (1912), *A Chinese-English Dictionary*, second edition, revised and enlarged, Shanghai and London.

Goto, T. (1956), 'Mongoruzoku ni okeru obo no sūhai sono bunka ni okeru sho kinō' (The worship of obo among the Mongols and its cultural functions). *Minzokugaku Kenkyū*, vol. 20 (August 1956), pp.47-71.

Haenisch, E. (1937-9), *Manghol un niuca tobca'an* (Yüan ch'ao pi shi). Geheime Geschichte der Mongolen. Aus der chinesischen Transkription . . . im mongolischen Wortlaut wiederhergestellt, Leipzig, second edition, 1962.

Haenisch, E. (1941), *Die Geheime Geschichte der Mongolen: Aus einer mongolischen Niederschrift des Jahres 1240 von der Insel Kode'e im*

Keluren-Fluss erstmalig übersetzt und erläutert, Leipzig, second edition, 1948.

Haltod, M. (1966), 'Ein Schamanengesang aus dem Bulgan-Gebiet', in Heissig, 1966b, pp.71-9.

Hamada, K. and Mizuro, S. (1938), 'Hung-shan Ho, Ch'ih-Feng', *Archaeologia Orientalis*, Series A, vols 4 and 6.

Hansen, H. H. (1950), *Mongol Costumes* (Nationalmuseets Skrifter, Etnografisk Raekke, 3), Copenhagen.

Harlez, C. J. de (1887), *La Religion nationale des Tartares Orientaux, Mandchous et Mongols, comparée à la religion des anciens Chinois, d'après les textes indigènes*, Brussels.

Hattori, S. (1940), 'The Mongolian Documents found at Olon Süme', *Tōhō Gakuhō'*, vol. 11 (in Japanese).

Heissig, W. (1944), 'Schamanen und Geisterbeschwörer im Küriye-Banner', *Folklore Studies* (Peking), vol. 3.

Heissig, W. (1946), 'Bolur Erike, "Eine Kette aus Bergkristallen", eine Mongolische Chronik der Kienlung-zeit, von Rasipungsγ (1774-5); literatur-historisch untersucht', Peiping (Monumenta Serica, Monograph 10, Fu-jen University).

Heissig, W. (1950a), 'Marginalien zur Ordos-chronik *Subud erike* (1835), *Zeitschrift der Deutschen Morgenländischen Gesellschaft*, vol. 100, pp.600-17.

Heissig, W. (1950b), 'A contribution to the knowledge of East Mongolian folk poetry', *Folklore Studies*, vol. 9, pp.153-78.

Heissig, W. (1953), 'A Mongolian source to the Lamaist suppression of shamanism in the 17th century', *Anthropos*, vol. 48, pp.1-29 and 493-536.

Heissig, W. (1953-4), 'Neyiči toyin, Das Leben eines lamaistisches Mönches (1557-1653), aus seiner mongolischen Biographie übersetzt und mit einer Einleitung', *Sinologica*, vol. 3 (1953) and vol. 4 (1954).

Heissig, W. (1954a), 'Die Pekinger lamaistischen Blockdrucke in mongolischer Sprache; Materialien zur mongolischen Literaturgeschichte', Wiesbaden (Göttinger asiatische Forschungen, 2).

Heissig, W. (1954b), 'Zur geistigen Leistung der neubekehrten Mongolen des späten 16. und frühen 17. Jh.', *Ural-Altaische Jahrbücher*, vol. 26, pp. 101-16.

Heissig, W. (1955), *Ostmongolische Reise*, Darmstadt.

Heissig, W. (1959a), *Die Familien- und Kirchengeschichtsschreibung der Mongolen*, Part I, 16.-18. Jh. Wiesbaden (Asiatische Forschungen, 5).

Heissig, W. (1959b), 'Mongolisches Schrifttum im Linden-Museum', *Tribus*, vol. 8, pp. 39-56.

Heissig, W. (1959c), *Altan Kürdün Mingγan Gegesütü Bičig*. Eine Mongolische Chronik von Siregetü Guosi Dharma (1739) herausgegeben und mit Einleitung und Namensverzeichnis versehen, Copenhagen (Monumenta Linguarum Asiae Maioris, Seria Nova, Band I).

Heissig, W. (1961a), *Erdeni-yin erike*, Mongolische Chronik der Lamaistische Klosterbauten der Mongolei von Isibalden (1835), Copenhagen (Monumenta Linguarum Asiae Maioris, Seria Nova, Band II).

Heissig, W. (1961b), *Mongolische Handschriften, Blockdrucke, Landkarte*, Beschrieben von Walther Heissig unter Mitarbeit von Klaus Sagaster.

Wiesbaden (Verzeichnis der orientalischen Handschriften in Deutschland, herausgegeben von Wolfgang Voigt. Band I).

Heissig, W. (1962a), *Beiträge zur Übersetzungsgeschichte des mongolischen buddhistischen Kanons*, Göttingen (Abhandlungen der Akademie der Wissenschaften in Göttingen, philologisch-historische Klasse, 3. Folge, Nr. 50.)

Heissig, W. (1962b), *Helden-, Höllenfahrts-und Schelmengeschichten der Mongolen*, aus dem Mongolischen übersetzt, Zürich (Manesse Bibliothek der Weltliteratur).

Heissig, W. (1963a), Eine kleine mongolische Klosterbibliothek aus Tsakhar, *Jahrbuch des Bernischen Historischen Museums*, 1961-2. (41/42 Jg.), pp.557-90, Berne.

Heissig, W. (1963b), *Mongolische Volksmärchen*. Aus dem Mongolischen übersetzt und mit einem Nachwort, Düsseldorf (Die Märchen der Weltliteratur).

Heissig, W. (1964), 'Ein Ms.-Fragment zum Kult der Dayisud-un Tngri und andere mongolische Fragmente im Ethnographischen Museum Antwerpen', *Central Asiatic Journal*, vol. 9 (September 1964), pp. 190-202.

Heissig, W. (1965a), 'Innermongolischen Arbeiten zur mongolischen Literaturgeschichte und Folkloreforschung', *Zeitschrift der Deutschen Morgenländischen Gesellschaft*, vol. 115, pp.153-99.

Heissig, W. (1959b), *Die Familien- und Kirchengeschichtsschreibung der Mongolen*, Part II, Section 1. Vier Chroniken des 19. Jahrhunderts in Facsimilia mit einer Einleitung und Namenregister, Wiesbaden (Asiatische Forschungen, Bd. 16).

Heissig, W. (1966a), *Mongolische volksreligiöse und folkloristische Texte aus europäischen Bibloteken*, mit einer Einleitung und Glossar, Wiesbaden (Verzeichnis der orientalischen Handschriften in Deutschland, Supplementband, 6).

Heissig, W. (1966b) (ed.), *Collectanea Mongolica*, Festschrift für Professor Dr. Rintchen zum 60. Geburtstag, Wiesbaden (Asiatische Forschungen, Bd. 17).

Heissig, W. (1966c), 'Zur Frage der Homogenität des ostmongolischen Schamanismus', in Heissig, 1966b, pp.81-100.

Heissig, W. (1966d), *Die mongolische Steininschrift und Manuskriptfragmente aus Olon süme in der Inneren Mongolei*, Göttingen (Abhandlungen der Akademie der Wissenschaften in Göttingen, philologisch-historische Klasse, 3. Folge, Nr. 63).

Heissig, W. (1968a), 'Lubsangcondans Darstellung des ostmongolischen Brauchtums', *Zentralasiatische Studien*, vol. 2, pp.211-63.

Heissig, W. (1968b), 'Zwölf Zeremonialtexte zue Stutenaussonderung aus Qanggin (Ordus) (Faksimilia)', *Zentralasiatische Studien*, vol. 2, pp.265-305.

Heissig, W. (1974), 'Ein innermongolisches Gebet sum Ewigen Himmel', *Zentralasiatische Studien*, vol. 8, pp.525-61.

Heissig, W. (1976), Eine Anrufung des 'Weissen Alten' in der Staatsbibliothek Preussischer Kulturbesitz Berlin. In H. Franke, W. Heissig, W. Treue (eds.), *Folia Rara* (Verzeichnis der Orientalischen Handschriften in Deutschland, Supplementband, 19), pp.51-61.

BIBLIOGRAPHY

Hoffmann, H. (1950), *Quellen zur Geschichte der Bon-Religion*, Wiesbaden.
Horloo, P. (1960), *Mongol ardyn jawgan ülger*, Ulanbator.
Hummel, S. (1959), 'Eurasiatische Traditionen in der tibetischen Bon-Religion', in *Opuscula Ethnologica Memoriae Ludovici Bíró Sacra*, Budapest.
Hummel, S. (1960), 'Der Weisse Alte (ein tibetische Bild)', *Sinologica*, vol. 6, no. 3, pp.193-206.
Huth, G. (1893-96), *Geschichte des Buddhismus in der Mongolei, aus dem tibetischen des Jigs-med nam-mk'a herausgegeben, übersetzt und erläutert*, Strasbourg.
Inaba, S. (1963), 'The Lineage of the Sa skya pa, A Chapter of the Red Annals', *Memoirs of the Toyo Bunko*, vol. 22, pp.107-25.
Jahn, K. (1956), 'Kamālashrī-Rashīd al-Dīn's "Life and Teaching of Buddha". A Source for the Buddhism of the Mongol Period', *Central Asiatic Journal*, vol. 2, pp.81-128.
Jimba, T. (1958), 'Irügel. qariyal. maγtaγal yojulal-un tuqai', *Mongyol teüke kele bičig*, vol. 4.
Kazakevich, B. A. (1934), *Sovremennennaya mongol'skaya toponymika*, Leningrad (Trudy Mongol'skoy Komisii, 13).
Kiselev, S. V. (1951), *Drevnyaya istoriya Yuzhnoy Sibiri*, Moscow.
Kiselev, S. V. (1965), *Drevnomongol'skie goroda* (Avtorskii kollektiv: S.V. Kiselev i dr.), Moscow.
Kler, J. (1957), 'Die Windpferdfahne oder das K'i-Mori bei den Ordos-Mongolen', *Oriens*, vol. 10, pp.90-106.
Kudryavtsev, F. A. (1940), *Istoriya buryat-mongol'skogo maroda* (l. Ot XVII v. do 60-kh godov XIX v.), Moscow.
Lattimore, O. (1941), *Mongol Journeys*, London.
Lattimore, O. reference to journal *Pacific Affairs*.
Laufer, B. (1907), 'Skizze der mongolischen Literatur', *Keleti Szemle*, vol. 8, pp.165-261 (Budapest).
Lessing, F. D. (1935), *Mongolen; Hirten, Priester und Dämonen*, Berlin.
Lessing, F. D. (1942), *Yung-ho-kung; An Iconography of the Lamaist Cathedral in Peking with Notes on Lamaist Mythology and Cult*, vol. 1. (Sino-Swedish Expedition, vol. 8, part 1), Stockholm.
Löwenthal, R. (transl.), (1955), *The Mongol Chronicles of the Seventeenth Century by C. Z. Zamcarano*, Wiesbaden (Göttinger asiatische Forschungen, 3).
Lüdtke, W. (1927), Die Verehrung Tschingis-Chans bei den Ordos-Mongolen. Nach dem Berichte G. M. Potanins aus dem Russischen übersetzt und erläutert, *Archiv für Religionswissenschaft*, vol. 25, pp. 83-129.
Maiskii, I. M. (1929), *Sovremennaya Mongoliya*. Irkutsk.
Mándoki, L. (1963), 'Asiatische **Sternnamen**', in Diószegi (1963), pp.523-30.
Manijab (1957), 'Soyol-un öb-i asiγlaqu tuqai jöblelge', *Mongyol kele bičiq*.
Miller, R. J. (1959), *Monasteries and Culture Change in Inner Mongolia*. Wiesbaden (Asiatische Forschungen, Bd. 2).
Mostaert, A. (1934), *Ordosica*. Peking (reprint from Bulletin No. 9 (1934) of the Catholic University of Peking).
Mostaert, A. (1935), ' "L'Ouverture du sceau" et les adresses chez les Ordos', *Monumenta Serica*, vol. 1, no. 2, pp.315-37.
Mostaert, A. (1937),'Textes oraux ordos, recuellis et publiés', Peking (*Monumenta Serica*, Monograph series, No. 1).

Mostaert, A. (1949), *Folklore ordos; traduction des Textes oraux ordos*, Peking (*Monumenta Serica*, Monograph series, No. 11).

Mostaert, A. (1956), 'Matériaux éthnographiques relatifs aux Mongols ordos', *Central Asiatic Journal*, vol. 2, no. 4, pp.241-94.

Mostaert, A. (1957a), 'Note sur le culte du Viellard blanc chez les Ordos', *Studia Altaica*, Festschrift für Nikolaus Poppe, pp.108-17, Wiesbaden.

Mostaert, A. (1957b), 'Le mot Natigay/Nacigai chez Marco Polo', *Oriente Poliano*, pp.95-101, Rome.

Mostaert, A. (1957c), 'Sur le culte de Sayang secen et de son bisaioul Qutuqtai secen chez les Ordos', *Harvard Journal of Asiatic Studies*, vol. 20, pp.534-66.

Mostaert, A. (1962), 'A propos d'une prière au feu', in Poppe, N. (ed.), *American Studies in Altaic linguistics*, pp.191-223, Bloomington, Indiana (Uralic and Altaic Series, vol. 13).

Mostaert, A. and Cleaves, F. W. (1956), 'Erdeni-yin tobci by Sayang secen', with a critical introduction by A. Mostaert and an editor's foreword by F. W. Cleaves, Cambridge, Mass. (Harvard-Yenching Institute, Scripta Mongolica, No. 2).

Mostaert, A. and Cleaves, F. W. (1959), *Bolor erike by Rasipungsuy*, Mongolian chronicle with a critical introduction by A. Mostaert and an editor's foreword by F. W. Cleaves, Cambridge, Mass. (Harvard-Yenching Institute, Scripta Mongolica, No. 3), 5 vols.

Mostaert, A. and Cleaves, F. W. (1962), *Les Lettres de 1289 et 1305 des ilkhan Aryun et Oljeitü à Philippe le Bel*, Cambridge, Mass. (Harvard-Yenching Institute, Scripta Mongolica, Monograph Series).

Moule, A. C. and Pelliot, P. (1938), *Marco Polo, The Description of the World*, translated and annotated, London, vol. I.

Nasambaljir, C. (1960), *Erdeni-yin erike*, by Galdan, Ulan Bator (Institutum Historiae, Monumenta Historica, vol. 3).

Nebesky-Wojkowitz, R. de (1956), *Oracles and Demons of Tibet*, 'S-Gravenhage.

Oshibuchi, H. (1952), 'Shoki mōko minzoku no hi ni kansuru fūshū ni tsuite' (On customs relating to fire of the early Mongols), *Jimbun Kenkyū* III/7.

Pallas, P. S. (1776-1801), *Sammlungen historischer Nachrichten über die Mongolischen Völkerschaften*, St Petersburg, 2 vols.

Pallisen, N. (1949), 'Die alte Religion des mongolischen Volkes und die Geschichte des Verhältnisses der Mongolen zu anderen Religionen während der Herrschaft der Tschingisiden', Marburg, (Inaug. Diss).

Partanen, F. (trans.) (1941), 'A description of Buriat shamanism', *Journal de la Societé Finno-Ougrienne* (Helsinki), vol. 51.

Poppe, N. N. (1925), 'Zum Feuerkultus bei den Mongolen', *Asia Maior*, vol. 2, pp.130-45.

Poppe, N. N. (1932a), 'Opisanie mongol'skikh "shamanskikh" rukopisey Instituta Vostokovedeniya', *Zapiski Instituty Vostokovedeniya Akademii Nauk SSSR*, vol. 1, pp.151-210.

Poppe, N. N. (1932b), *Proizvedeniya narodnoy slovesnosti khalkha-mongolov*, III, Leningrad.

Poppe, N. N. (1935), *Letopisi khorinskikh buryat*, Leningrad (Trudy Institut Vostokovedeniya Akademii Nauk, No. 9).

Poppe, N. N. (1936), *Letopisi selenginskikh buryat,* Leningrad (Trudy Institut Vostokovedeniya Akademii Nauk, No. 12).

Poppe, N. N. (1955), *Mongolische Volksdichtung; Sprüche, Lieder, Märchen und Heldensagen, /khalkha-mongolische Texte mit deutscher ubersetzung, einer Einleitung und Anmerkungen,* Wiesbaden (Akademie der Wissenschaften und der Literatur, Veröffentlichungen der orientalischen Kommission, No. 7).

Poppe, N. N. (1957), *The Mongolian Monuments in ḥPhags-pa-Script,* second edition, translated and edited by J. R. Krueger, Wiesbaden (Göttinger Asiatische Forschungen, Bd. 8).

Potanin, G. N. (1881-3), *Ocherki Severo-Zapadnoi Mongolii, Resul'taty puteshestviya ispolnennogo v 1867-77 godakh po porucheniyu Imperatorskago Russkago Geograficheskago Obshchestva,* St Petersburg, 4 vols.

Potanin, G. N. (1893), *Tangutsko-Tibetskaya okraina Kitaya i Tsentral'naya Mongoliya,* St Petersburg, 2 vols.

Poucha, P. (1956), *Die Geheime Geschichte der Mongolen, als Geschichtsquelle und Literaturdenkmal. Ein Beitrag zu ihrer Erklärung,* Prague. (*Archiv orientalni,* Supplementa, No. 4).

Pozdneyev, A. M. (1887), *Ocherki byta buddiiskikh monastyrei i buddiiskago dukhovensta v Mongolii,* St Petersburg (Zapiski Imperatorskago Russkago Geograficheskago Obshchestva no otdeleniyu etnografii, No. 16).

Pozdneyev, A. M. (1896-1898), *Mongoliya i Mongoly. Resul'taty poezdki v Mongoliyu, ispolnennoi v 1892-1893 gg.,* St Petersburg, 2 vols.

Pozdneyev, A. M. (1900), *Mongol'skaya Khrestomatiya dlya pervonachal'nago prepodavaniya,* St Petersburg.

Rinchen, B. (1953), *Üür-ün tuya* (Rays of the Rising Sun), historical novel. Second edition (vol. 2), Peking.

Rinchen, B. (1955), 'A propos du chamanisme mongol (Le culte de l'ongon Dayan degereki chez les Mongols . . .)', *Studia Orientalia (Fennica),* vol. 18, no. 4, pp.8-16.

Rinchen, B. (1958a), 'En Marge du culte de Guesser Khan en Mongolie', *Journal de la Societe Finno-Ougrienne,* vol. 60, pp.1-51.

Rinchen, B. (1958b), 'Schamanistische Geister der Gebirge Dörben aɣula-yin eǰen in Urgaer Pantomimen', *Acta Ethnographica Academiae Scientiarum Hungaricae,* vol. 6.

Rinchen, B. (1959), 'Zum Kult Tschinggis-Khans bei den Mongolen: Opferlieder Tayilɣa-yin da un', in *Opuscula Ethnologica Memoriae Ludovici Bíró Sacra,* pp.9-22, Budapest.

Rinchen, B. (1959-61), *Matériaux pour l'étude du chamanisme mongol,* I: Souces littéraires; II: Textes chamanistes bouriates, Wiesbaden (Asiatische Forschungen, Bd. 3 and Bd. 8).

Rinchen, B. (1960), 'Nomči qatun's version of Kesar Saga', *Corpus Scriptorum Mongolorum,* IX, fasc. 4a.

Risch, F. (1930), *Johann de Plano Carpini, Geschichte der Mongolen und Reisebericht 1245-1247,* Leipzig.

Rock, J. F. (1952), *The Na-Khi Naga cult and related ceremonies,* Rome.

Roerich, G. N. (1942), 'The epic of King Kesar of Ling', *Journal of the Royal Asiatic Society of Bengal,* vol. 8.

Sagaster, K. (1960), 'Ñag dbaṅ blo bzaṅ č'os ldan (1642-1714). Leben und historische Bedeutung des 1 (Pekinger) lCaṅ skya Khutukhtu, dargestellt an Hand seiner mongolischen Biographie Subud Erike und andere Quellen', Bonn (thesis).

Sagaster, K. (1966), 'Ein Dokument des Tschinggis-Khan-Kults in der Khalkha-Mongolei', in Heissig (1966b), pp.193-234.

Sagaster, K. (1967), *Ńag Dbaṅ blo bzaṅ č'os ldan. Subud erike, ein Rosenkranz aus Perlen. Die Biographie des 1. Pekinger lCaṅ skya Khutukhtu*, Herausgegeben, übersetzt und kommentiert, Wiesbaden (Asiatische Forschungen, Bd. 20).

Sandschejew, G. D.(=Sanzheyev) (1927), 'Weltanschauung und Schamanismus der Alaren-Burjaten', *Anthropos*, vol. 22. pp.576-613 and 933-55.

Schmidt, I. J. (=Shmidt, I. I.) (1829). *Geschichte der Ost-Mongolen und ihres Fürstenhauses verfasst von Ssanang Ssetsen Chungtaidschi der Ordus*, St Petersburg and Leipzig (reprinted, The Hague, 1961).

Schmidt, W. (1952), *Der Ursprung der Gollesidee. Eine historisch-kritische und positive Studie*, Münster (references are to vol. 10=Die Religionen der Hirtenvölker, IV).

Schröder, D. (1952), 'Zur Religion der Turjen des Sininggebietes (Kukunor)', *Anthropos*, vol. 47, pp.1-79, 620-58 and 822-70.

Schubert, J. (1966), 'Ein Ritual für die Berggottheit des K'engtei Xaġan', in Heissig (1966b), pp.235-47.

Serruys, P. (1945), *Pei-lou fong-sou, Les Coutumes des Esclaves Septentrionaux de Hsiao Ta-heng, Monumenta Serica*, vol. 10, pp.117-208.

Sodnam, B. (1962), 'Mongolyn haryn böögijn duudlagyn tuhaj', *Studia Mongolica* (Ulan Bator), vol. 4, fasc. 3.

Stein, R. A. (1959), *Recherches sur l'epopée et le barde au Tibet*, Paris.

Sugiyama, I. (1940), 'Naiman-chi ni okeru zōkyō to shuzoku', *Mōko Kenkyu*, vol. 2, no. 4(?), pp.64-77.

Thiel, J. (1961), 'Der Streit der Buddhisten und Taoisten zur Mongolenzeit', *Monumenta Serica*, vol. 20.

Torii, R. (1942), *Sculptured Stone Tombs of the Liao Dynasty*. Peking.

Tucci, G. (1949), *Tibetan Painted Scrolls*, Rome, 3 vols.

Unkrig, W. A. (1927), *Dhyana und Samadhi im mongolischen Lamaismus*, Hannover.

Vladimirtsov, B. Y. (1924), 'O prozvishche "Dayan"-qaγan', *Doklady Rossiiskoi Akademii Nauk*, Seria B, pp.119-21.

Vladimirtsov, B. Y. (1948), *Le Régime social des Mongols. Le feodalisme nomade* (Translated from the Russian) (Publications du Musee Guimet, Bibliothèque d'étude, vol. 52).

Weber, M. (1923), *Gesammelte Aufsätze zur Religionssoziologie*, vol. II, Tübingen.

Wright, A. F. (1948), 'Fo-t'u-teng: a biography', *Harvard Journal of Asiatic Studies*, vol. 11, pp.321-71.

Wyngaert, A. von den (1929), *Sinica Franciscana*, vol. 1. Quaracchi-Florence.

Ysbrants-Ides, E. (1704), *Driejaarige reize naar China, te lande gedaan*, Amsterdam.

Yule, H. and Cordier, H. (1903), *The Book of Ser Marco Polo, the Venetian*, *concerning the Kingdoms and Marvels of the East,* translated by H. Yule. Third edition, revised throughout in the light of recent discoveries by H. Cordier, London, 2 vols.

Zhamtsarano, Ts. (1913), *Poezdka v yuzhnuyu Mongoliyu 1909-1910 gg.* St Petersburg (Izvestiya Russkago komiteta dlya izcučniya sredney i vostochnoi Azii, Ser. 2).

Zhamtsarano, Ts. (1936), *Mongol'skie letopisi XVII veka,* Moskow and Leningrad (Trudy Institut Vostokovedeniya Akademii Nauk, No. 16).

INDEX